PhanFood

Illustration: Cody Schibi

PhanFood

From the Kitchen Pot to the Tour Lot

Edited By Taraleigh Weathers and Pete Mason

excelsior editions

An imprint of State University of New York Press
www.sunypress.edu

Front cover illustration ©2010 Cody Schibi.
Back cover illustration ©2010 AJ Masthay.

Published by
State University of New York Press, Albany

Printed in the United States of America

For information, address State University of New York Press, Albany, NY
www.sunypress.edu

Production by Kelli W. LeRoux
Marketing by Michael Campochiaro

Library of Congress Cataloging-in-Publication Data

Phanfood : from the kitchen pot to the tour lot / edited by Taraleigh Weathers and Pete Mason.
p. cm.
Prepared for and by fans of the rock band Phish.
Includes index.
ISBN 978-1-4384-3668-5 (alk. paper) -- ISBN 978-1-4384-3669-2
1. Outdoor cooking. 2. Cooking, American. 3. Tailgate parties. 4. Picnics.
5. Cookbooks. I. Weathers, Taraleigh. II. Mason, Pete. III. Phish (Musical group)

TX823.P456 2010
641.5'78--dc22 2010037244

10 9 8 7 6 5 4 3 2 1

This book is dedicated to

Phish, their phans and the city of Burlington, Vermont; Peter and Theresa Mason, for teaching Pete to cook a variety of foods from the family cookbook; Dan Weathers for being an awesome husband and for giving Taraleigh someone special to cook for; Renee and Joe Silberberg for allowing and supporting Taraleigh to be herself; and Joshua Rosenthal for showing Taraleigh that cooking is simple and that she can do anything.

All net profits from the sale of this book will benefit the food pantries and local charities of the towns Phish plays during each tour as well as Phish's hometown Burlington, VT.

Contents

Introduction

The idea of Phanfood came to me when I was walking on the bike path in Burlington, VT. I had wanted to do some sort of cookbook for some time when the idea just popped into my head…a cookbook for Phish fans, by Phish fans that benefits people who can't afford to eat delicious meals themselves. PhanArt Pete Mason immediately came to mind as a collaborator for the cookbook since he was so successful with his PhanArt book. I called him immediately and spurted out my idea to him and he loved it as much as I did! We set the wheels in motion right away. Pete set us up with Julie Parker who designed our logo and website. We decided to donate money to the food pantries in the towns where Phish tours most. Talented Phish artists were interested in providing us with artwork. Britt Nemeth signed on as the graphic artist in charge of the layout. Recipes starting coming in and we were on our way to a kick-ass book that is going to help so many people eat delicious foods! You know how when you are supposed to do something and are on the right path, things just seem to happen? All the right people want to help you and things just fall in line? Well that is what happened for us and for PhanFood! ~Taraleigh Weathers

Special Thanks

Britt, Dan, Julie, artists Cody Schibi, AJ Masthay, and Ryan Kerrigan, and everyone who submitted recipes; Greg Bell, Phish, The Heavy Pets, The McLovins, Headcount, and everyone who is going to cook up something fabulous after reading this book. Special thanks to Kelli Williams-LeRoux and everyone at SUNY Press, Jonathan Schwartz, Joshua Rosenthal, Renee and Jose Silberberg, Peter and Theresa Mason, Amy Fischer, Tim O'Shea, Oprah Winfrey, Tom Hanks, and Warren Zevon.

Appetizers and Soups

Name: Bo, the "EAT MORE KALE" guy

Location: Vermont

Occupation: Foster parent/t-shirt artist

Shows Attended: 50

Favorite Song: "Reba"

Favorite Experience: Front row center seats, Fox Theatre, Atlanta, Georgia

Origin of recipe: My wife and I tinkered with an old standard recipe to "make it ours."

Favorite memory of sharing recipe: Showing how yummy kale can be, when done right.

Song this recipe is: "Velvet Sea"

Show this recipe is: It would be a good one.

Bobo's Pesto

Ingredients:
1 bunch KALE (any variety will do)
2 cups fresh basil leaves, packed
½ cup freshly grated Parmesan-Reggiano or Romano cheese
½ cup extra virgin olive oil
⅓ cup pine nuts or walnuts
3 medium-sized garlic cloves, minced
Salt and freshly ground black pepper to taste

Directions:
1. Wash and steam the KALE until tender.
2. Combine the KALE and basil with the pine nuts, and pulse a few times in a food processor. (If you are using walnuts instead of pine nuts and they are not already chopped, pulse them a few times first, before adding the KALE and basil.) Add the garlic, and pulse a few times more.
3. Slowly add the olive oil in a constant stream while the food processor is on. Stop to scrape down the sides of the food processor with a rubber spatula. Add the grated cheese and pulse again until blended. Add a pinch of salt and freshly ground black pepper to taste.

Makes 2 cups.

Serve with pasta, or over baked potatoes, or spread over toasted baguette slices.

Serves: 4

Appetizers and Soups

Name: Chris Ott

Location: Follansbee, West Virginia

Occupation: Kitchen Manager

Shows Attended: 29

Favorite Song: "Tube"

Favorite Experience: Big Cypress was unbelievable! Phantasy land to say the least. Ferris wheel, NYE antics, amazing art, crazy late-night jams, a six-hour-plus set, need I say more?

Origin of recipe: My father, Tim Ott, invented this Cream of Morel Soup recipe a long time ago. Hailing from West Virginia, our family knows how to "live off the land." Harvesting the morel mushroom, a choice wild edible, is a favorite pastime of my family and others in our region. Combining a cream-based soup with this delicious fungus was a no-brainer.

Favorite memory of sharing recipe: I once prepared this for famous mycologists David Fischer and Chris Matherley, and many others at a mushroom foray that I helped lead. Everyone was blown away! They all had mushroom soup before, which made me realize that this recipe was a cut above the rest. It is now prepared at all of Matherley's forays.

Song this recipe is: "Moma Dance." Like the funk in this song, the flavor hits you right off the bat.

Show this recipe is: 12/7/1997 Dayton, Ohio.
Like the soup, this show is delectable to say the least. While there are no 30 minute jams or guest appearances, this show, like the soup, stands above the rest because of its depth of tastiness and smooth finish (not to mention the "Tube Reprise Funk Jam" that is outstanding, along with Slave).

You Enjoy My Soup

Ingredients:

Soup

½ pound morel mushrooms (any store-bought mushroom will do)
⅔ stick butter
1 pint heavy cream
1 tablespoon sea salt
1 teaspoon ground black pepper
1 teaspoon dried tarragon

Garnish

4 thin slices toasted baguette bread
1 tablespoon extra virgin olive oil
1 tablespoon finely diced green onion

Directions:

Place ⅓ stick of butter in a sauté pan. Raise temperature till butter starts to brown (not smoke). Add morels (preferably), or substitute any store-bought mushroom. After 2 minutes, lower temp to medium and continue to brown mushrooms. Once mushroom browning is evident, kick down burner temp to medium-low. Add all heavy cream and spices. Bring to a simmer. Add remaining (⅓ stick) butter. Proceed with a slow simmer and occasionally stir.

While the soup is consummating, toast your sliced baguette. Then drizzle with the tablespoon of olive oil. Place the crostini in the four bowls at an angle so that the bread will be exposed after pouring the soup in the bowl. Ladle soup into the four bowls. Top with the green blast of the onion. Then, You Enjoy My Soup.

Serves: 4

Appetizers and Soups

Name: Lindsay Jones

Location: Utica, NY

Occupation: Underwriter

Shows Attended: 27

Favorite Song: "Carini"

Favorite Experience: My roadtrip to Alpine Valley this year!

Origin of recipe: Modified from a recipe I found in an old cookbook.

Favorite memory of sharing recipe: I made it for a "food day" at work; it was a big hit!

Potato Cheddar Chowder

Ingredients:
¼ pound bacon
¼ cup butter
1 cup heavy cream
2 small leeks, diced
1 large onion, diced
1 carrot, diced
1 clove garlic, minced
½ cup flour
6 cups chicken stock
3 pounds white potatoes, cut into ½ inch cubes
1 pound shredded cheddar (as sharp as you like)
⅓ teaspoon salt
¼ teaspoon pepper

Directions:
1. In a large pot, cook the bacon under medium heat. Leave 1 to 2 tablespoons of the drippings in the bottom, and remove the bacon. The bacon is going to be used as a garnish, so feel free to snack on it as you cook. Add the butter and let it melt. Add in the diced leeks, onions, carrots and garlic. Let them cook until soft. Stir in the flour. Slowly stir in the broth. Add in the cubed potatoes and bring the whole mixture up to a boil. Turn it down to low, cook for about 15 minutes or until the potatoes are done and the broth is thick.
2. Put the cheddar cheese in a large bowl. Take about ¼ of the hot broth and pour into the bowl, mixing in and melting the cheese. Once it's all melted, put the cheese mixture back into the large pot.
3. Mix in the heavy cream on medium high heat. Add salt and pepper to taste.
4. Serve with bacon and cheese on top (assuming there is still bacon).

Serves: 20

Appetizers and Soups

Name: Loren Marcus

Location: Minneapolis, MN

Occupation: Swimming Pool Curator

Shows Attended: 14

Favorite Song: "Run Like An Antelope"

Favorite Experience: Coventry. The time in my life I felt most alive.

Origin of recipe: Mike told me it was healthy.

Favorite memory of sharing recipe: A 300 pound Offensive lineman from Iowa State claiming he was going to lose 100 pounds from the recipe. I wished him luck.

Song this recipe is: "Harry Hood"

Show this recipe is: '98 Halloween set. When it started folks were unsure, but by the end it was crispy and delicious.

I'm Baked, I'm Broccoli

Ingredients:
Broccoli florets
Extra virgin olive oil
Salt
Pepper

Directions:

1. Pre-heat oven to 425 degrees.
2. Chop broccoli and arrange on baking sheet.
3. Drizzle with extra virgin olive oil.
4. Add salt and pepper.

Bake at 425 degrees for 30 minutes

Serves: 2

Appetizers and Soups

Name: Mark Florczyk

Location: Cheshire, Massachusetts

Occupation: Corporate Mogul

Shows Attended: 60+

Favorite Song: "My Friend, My Friend"

Favorite Experience: Walking into Great Woods back in '95 just knowing something special was going on… either that or watching it snow inside MSG on NYE!

Origin of recipe: The best bar in town. This is their wing recipe. It rules.

Favorite memory of sharing recipe: Getting told it looks like crap by PT!

Song this recipe is: "The Went's Bathtub Gin"

Guata Wings!

Ingredients:
5 ounces soy sauce
5 ounces red hot
2 ounces vegetable oil
2 ounces honey or molasses
⅛ tablespoon granulated garlic
⅛ tablespoon ground ginger

Directions:
1. Throw 12 wings or so on the grill at 350 to 400 degrees.
2. When they start to get marked up (usually around 5 to 6 minutes or so) flip them over.
3. Take them inside and put them in a big mixing bowl.
4. Dump in the sauce mixture.
5. Mix them all together.
6. Enjoy.

Serves: 2

Appetizers and Soups

Name: Matthew Andress

Location: Miami, FL

Occupation: Art Bureaucrat

Shows Attended: 21

Favorite Song: "Fly Famous Mockingbird"

Favorite Experience: Deercreek 6/24/2004: During the set break, squeezing through the area between the amphitheatre and the bathrooms where a true traffic jam was happening. It was so jam packed, shoulder to shoulder, that you could only put down one foot at a time. The whole mass of people was walking as one being. Everyone was talking, laughing and enjoying the mess. It will forever be known to me and my companions as the Vacuum.

Origin of recipe: The soup was originally from a vegetarian cookbook. After years of fine tuning, this is how it is consistently made these days. It is a simple soup that always seems to hit the spot.

Favorite memory of sharing recipe: I love making this soup for my wife Lia; it is one of her favorite things that I make.

Song this recipe is: "Simple"

Show this recipe is: I think this soup is most like the acoustic set from Festival 8, 11/1/2009. No flashy lights or effects pedals. Just four guys, some instruments and a bunch of friends.

The Ambassadors' Zucchini Soup

Ingredients:
2 tablespoons olive oil
2 tablespoons butter
1 large onion, roughly chopped
2 pounds zucchini, sliced
2 tablespoons dried oregano or other herb
Salt and pepper (to taste)
3 cups stock
2 cups milk or cream
1 cup crumbled cheese of choice: feta, ricotta salata, goat (to serve)

Directions:
1. Heat butter and olive oil in deep dutch oven.
2. Sauté onion, oregano, salt and pepper.
3. Add zucchini and let cook well, about ten minutes.
4. Cover with the stock and bring to a boil.
5. Reduce heat and let simmer partially covered for 20 minutes.
6. Add milk and purée with immersion blender.

Serve with crumbled cheese on top.

Serves: 6

Appetizers and Soups

Name: Taraleigh Weathers

Location: Burlington, VT

Occupation: Magazine Maker/Holistic Health Counselor/Healthy Hippie

Shows Attended: Many

Favorite Song: "Tela"

Favorite Experience: One of my favorite experiences has to be at Phish Hampton 2009. We were all so excited! We didn't know what to expect. Were they going to suck? Would they be awesome? Before night one the anticipation was crazy. The lights went down and I just screamed at the top of my lungs. I felt like I was going to jump out of my skin and then the band busted into Fluffhead and I knew…the boys were back!

Origin of recipe: My husband, Dan, and I have potluck dinners at our house and many of our friends are vegetarians so I'm always thinking of new things to make that everyone will like…and who doesn't like balls?

Song this recipe is: When Fishman sang "I Kissed a Girl" in Saratoga.

Show this recipe is: I think it was in 2000 I saw Phish in Vegas, and then right after that I went to Phoenix.

Everyone was very tired, and I have to say that Phoenix show lacked some meat. It was very slow and relaxing, which I was happy about because I was soooooo tired.

Touch My Meatless Balls

Ingredients:
1 cup textured vegetable protein
¾ cup water
1 tablespoon tamari/soy sauce
1 tablespoon olive oil
1 cage-free egg
1 teaspoon oregano
1 teaspoon sea salt
2 cloves garlic chopped
½ cup breadcrumbs (I used gluten free)

Directions:

1. Preheat oven to 400 degrees.
2. Soak textured vegetable protein in water for 5 to 10 minutes in a large bowl.
3. Add in all ingredients.
4. Stir with a spatula or rice paddle until it looks like ground beef.
5. Make into golf-ball-sized balls.
6. Place on greased baking pan.
7. Cook for 15 minutes.
8. Flip.
9. Cook for additional 15 minutes.

Serving suggestions:
Spaghetti and "meat" balls
"Meat" ball parmesan
Swedish "meat" balls
Throw them at your lover

Name: Peach Robidoux

Location: Whately, MA

Occupation: Mama, Writer

Shows Attended: Hundreds

Favorite Song: "Run Like an Antelope"

Favorite Experience: My favorite experiences with Phish were when they were still a $2 band who played the Living Room on occasion when Max Creek was on vacation. I used to be able to stand up front or sometimes sit on the corner of the stage. Because I have red hair, I stand out, especially to other redheads. So, I always got eye contact and winks from Trey. We used to have contests to see how many band members we could get to wink at us.

Origin of recipe: This recipe is an adaptation of one from Jane Brody. I made it a little bit easier and with a snap of rum. This is a super-easy recipe you'll crave hereafter.

Favorite memory of sharing recipe: I made it for my in-laws and my family on a hot August day when my daughter was a baby. I remember sitting outside at a table with the baby on my lap, sipping this yummy cold soup and listening to the birds and the wind in the trees.

Song this recipe is: "Run Like an Antelope"

Show this recipe is: Townsend, VT, June 16, 1990. It was a warm day near the river with beautiful breezes blowing, the crowd was small and lovely, and it was a perfect early summer day for listening to Phish outside. This soup, with its cool, mellow, summery taste reminds me of that show—easy and sweet with a gorgeous "You Enjoy Myself" into "Run Like an Antelope," ending the second of three sets.

Run Like a Cantaloupe Soup

Ingredients:
2 ripe cantaloupes, seeded and flesh diced
4 tablespoons lemon juice
2 tablespoons rum (optional)

Directions:
1. In a blender or food processor, purée the cantaloupe with the lemon juice (and rum if desired) until smooth.
2. Refrigerate covered for at least 3 hours.
3. Serve with a sprig of mint.

Serves: 8

Appetizers and Soups

Name: Phil Kazlauskas

Location: Rhode Island

Occupation: Will be teaching in Korea in two months

Shows Attended: 35

Favorite Song: "Weekapaug Groove"

Favorite Experience: Lemonwheel with all 3 of my older brothers, or Worcester '98!!!

Origin of recipe: I basically got the idea for this recipe from a Mexican restaurant that would make the guacamole right in front of you. You got to select how much of what ingredient you wanted. It was delicious and I started making it all the time. This is how I like it. Change it and do what your palate wants!!!

Favorite memory of sharing recipe: I named it Fiesta Time because I bring this recipe to parties all the time. Every time I bring it people always rave about it, and it is always the first thing to be totally gone! If you bring this to a party people will praise you all night. I also had a Mexican woman tell me it was the best guacamole she'd ever had.

Song this recipe is: "Party Time"

Show this recipe is: Albany 11/28/09, because that show is when Phish became fresh again. And they opened with "Party Time."

Fiesta Time!

Ingredients:
3 avocados (about as soft as Fishman's butt in 1994)
2 tomatoes, gutted/diced
1 to 2 jalapeños
a handful of cilantro, minced (this is very important, so make sure it is SUPER fresh. I always eat a pinch of it in the store to make sure it is ok)
½ red onion
Salt (don't be shy)
Fresh lime juice

Optional:
Garlic (Usually I use this when I don't want to use the jalepeño. Also, I would get rid of the lime if you're going to use the garlic.)

Make sure these ingredients are all super fresh.

Directions:

1. Make sure you dice everything except the jalapeño nice and chunky.
2. Throw everything into a bowl and mix!!!
3. Taste it. If it needs more salt, cilantro, or jalapeños, throw it in there!

Serves: 6

Appetizers and Soups

Name: Yasemin Ipek

Location: Albany, NY

Occupation: Secretary

Shows Attended: 10

Favorite Song: How can I pick just one?!!

Favorite Experience: The 6/19/09 show in Indiana. Before they started playing there was a crazy storm brewing, and these intense lighting bolts started striking, but they weren't normal. They spiderwebbed into the clouds and never struck ground. Us New Yorkers are not used to that shit, haha. But anyway, when Phish started playing, the lightning started striking more, almost at each climax of the show. It had such an epic vibe.

Origin of recipe: My boyfriend has celiac disease, meaning he is gluten-free, which means that he can't have any wheat, rye, barley or basically anything breaded (this includes beer). He is absolutely in love with Phish (but hey, who isn't huh, haha). Anyway, we have been to a bunch of shows but he can never eat or drink anything on lot or at shows. So I felt bad and started trying to make my own gluten-free food, and came up with homemade quesadillas that are amazing!

Favorite memory of sharing recipe: The look on people's faces.

Fluffka Head Quesadilla

Ingredients:

<u>Tortilla Wrap</u> (gluten-free)
½ cup gluten-free flour
½ cup corn meal
A pinch of salt
1 egg
1 ½ cups water

<u>Quesadilla</u>
Grilled chicken
Onions
Peppers
Cheese
Anything else you would like to add

Directions:

1. Mix all wrap ingredients together until it mixes into a batter.
2. Put it on a hot plate pan and cook it like a pancake (the batter is supposed to be a bit thick).
3. Smooth it out to look round and flip it when you see the top start drying and the bottom lifting.
4. Slice up and cook the chicken, onions, peppers.
5. Add them to the tortilla wrap and melt the cheese!

Serves: 4

Appetizers and Soups

Name: Taraleigh Weathers

Location: Burlington, VT

Occupation: Magazine Maker/Holistic Health Counselor/Healthy Hippie

Shows Attended: Many

Favorite Song: "Tela"

Favorite Experience: I drove to Coventry with a friend and waited in 46 hours of traffic. Mike came on and announced that we should all turn around. I thought to myself, "Well…I'm just going to hike in." My ride had other plans and didn't want to leave me alone so he locked the doors and drove us all the way back to NJ. I was so upset. I wasn't going to miss these shows. I considered driving myself back. I knew that wasn't possible, so I decided to go to a movie theater to see the live simulcast. Everywhere was sold out but I found an extra in Philly. So I drove 3 hours and saw the shows in a theater. It was awesome! I felt like I was there. We had a glow-stick war, were yelling the songs we wanted to hear at the band, and we were dry. I loved it.

Origin of recipe: Sometimes you just need to feel grounded and rooted. What better way to do that than to eat a ton of root veggies!!

Favorite memory of sharing recipe: I make this a lot and everyone loves it. :)

Song this recipe is: "Slave to the Traffic Light"

Show this recipe is: Any of the shows at Red Rocks because even though that theater is at a very high altitude you feel grounded when you are there. Maybe it's just because I felt like I belonged there.

I Need to Feel Grounded After a Phish Show Root Veggie Bake

Ingredients:
4 carrots, chopped
4 parsnips, chopped
2 onions, chopped
4 cloves garlic, chopped
4 beets, peeled and chopped
2 sweet potatoes, chopped
2 potatoes, chopped
Olive oil
Sea salt
Pepper

You can add any other veggies that you choose as well.

Directions:
1. Preheat oven to 350 degrees.
2. Place all veggies in an oven safe baking dish.
3. Pour olive oil over all the veggies until there is a layer of oil on everything.
4. Sprinkle with sea salt, pepper, and any other seasonings you choose.
5. Bake for 45 minutes.

Serves: 8

Appetizers and Soups

Name: Nitti Sachdeva

Location: South Burlington, VT

Occupation: Business owner

Origin of recipe: A traditional family recipe.

Favorite memory of sharing recipe: On a cold evening with family.

Shows Attended: Summer Fancy Food Show NYC, DC Metropolitan Cooking Show.

Favorite Song: Indian classical and old Bollywood songs.

Favorite Experience: Talking about Deva Naturals Cooking.

Phish Songs: "Back On The Train" Becoz it reminds me of home.

Show this recipe is: I've never been to A Phish Show, but can't wait for my 1st.

Kaalae Cholae
(Black Chickpeas)

Ingredients:
2 cups black chickpeas
1 medium onion, chopped
3 cloves garlic, chopped
1 tablespoon ginger, minced
1 large tomato
2 cups water
2 tablespoons olive oil
Salt to taste
Deva Naturals Authentic Indian spice blend (Masala)
Cilantro for garnish

Directions:
1. Soak chickpeas overnight
2. Sauté all the above ingredients except chickpeas, water and cilantro to a soft golden brown.
3. Add the chickpeas with water and cook in a slow cooker all day, (5 to 7 hours) till soft or cook in a pressure cooker for 20 minutes on medium heat till soft.
4. Garnish with a few sprigs of fresh cilantro and salt.

Enjoy it piping hot with a side of steamed rice or bread!

More recipes: http://themangosteelady.blogspot.com

Serves: 4

Snacks

Name: Kate Zonis

Location: NYC

Occupation: Artist

Shows Attended: 30 or so

Favorite Song: "Halley's Comet," "Ya Mar," "Water in the Sky," "Split Open & Melt"

Favorite Experience: I suppose it was at Coventry, after hiking all those miles to get in. It was the last night and they were playing Down With Disease and everyone was throwing glowsticks and it was just so poignant. We'd put a tarp on the muddy ground and had a sacred space with some phans who'd been to countless shows and had real jobs. The guy was a fermentation microbiologist and the woman was a speech pathologist just so they could tour with Phish. Good crowd…the last couple miles of walking led us to a covered truck that was sneaking in loads of kids (who had tickets). Tons of us packed into the pitch black back of this big truck. They let us out just across the field from the venue and yelled RUN! It was my most authentic "illegal immigrant" experience. My father had also passed away just months before, and the whole thing was totally fortifying. To this day, I marvel at how well I was able to cope with his death, and it was largely thanks to Phish and the shows I'd been to in that period. (The previous year, IT was when my dad was ill,

and Phish also helped me cope with that so much.)

Origin of recipe: I made it up, baby!

Favorite memory of sharing recipe: As a vegetarian, I'd always been looked at with a skeptical eye by friends and family alike. They'd sigh, "Oh, what's Kate gonna try feeding us this time…" These tofu nuggets are liked by carnivore and herbivore alike. They are very nutritious, and are a great on-the-run kinda food.

Song this recipe is: "Lovin' Cup"

Show this recipe is: I'd say the second night at the recent MSG shows. Safe and fortifying, fulfilling and delicious. Full of favorite flavors.

Nut Encrusted Tofu Nuggets

Ingredients:
1 pound firm tofu
Approx. ½ cup sesame oil (or olive oil if you don't have sesame)
Approx. ⅓ cup soy sauce
1 cup almonds
1 cup seeds, whatever you've got. I like flax, sesame, pumpkin, and sunflower.
Lots of (1 cup or so) nutritional yeast
Squeeze of agave nectar or honey for dipping

Directions:

1. Throw nuts, seeds, and nutritional yeast in blender and make "breadcrumbs." You can leave them sorta big, or blend into a rough powder. Put them in a bowl.
2. Combine oil and soy sauce in a bowl and mix.
3. Cut tofu into relatively thin pieces; I like triangles because they're cute. Try for ½ inch thick.
4. Dip into liquid then into dry mixture. Sprinkle extra ample nutritional yeast on top.
5. Place on baking pan (oiled or with parchment paper) and bake at 350-375 degrees for 30 to 45 minutes.
6. Dip in agave or honey and ENJOY!

Serves: 4

Snacks

Name: Karen W.

Location: Philadelphia, PA

Occupation:

Shows Attended: 66

Favorite Song: "The Divided Sky"

Favorite Experience: Summer tour 98, west coast. My sister and I flew out with our camping equipment to Spokane on our way to the Gorge (we missed the Portland show) after I worked all day. We picked up our econo rental car and drove 1.5 hrs east instead of west (b.GPS) straight through Idaho into Montana in the middle of the night. When we realized it and turned around, we ended up camping at the Spokane KOA right outside of the airport because we were too tired to continue on to the Gorge that night. Nevertheless, the Gorge and subsequent shows through to Phoenix were incredible for us. So, as an experience, that is definitely the most memorable.

Recipe Name: Veggie hash featuring brussels sprouts

Origin of recipe: An adapted family recipe.

Favorite memory of sharing recipe: Eating it.

Song this recipe is: "Wading in a Velvet Sea"

Show this recipe is: Coventry - everything is minced.

Veggie Hash
Featuring Brussels Sprouts

Ingredients:
1 pound brussels sprouts, no stems, minced
1½ cups onions, minced
2 garlic cloves, minced
1 medium carrot, chopped fine
1 small zucchini or yellow squash, chopped fine
1 red or yellow bell pepper, seeded, minced
1 tablespoon olive oil
½ cup water
Sea salt and pepper to taste

Directions:
In a large sauté pan, heat olive oil over medium heat. Add onions and sauté about 5 mins until the onions are soft.

Add garlic, brussels sprouts and carrot to onions, then add the water and simmer the veggies, stirring occasionally about 7 mins or until water has completely evaporated. Stir in the zucchini/squash, bell pepper, salt and pepper to taste. Sauté another 2 minutes and serve.

Snacks

Name: Kevin Sullivan

Location: Rockville Centre, NY

Occupation: Finance

Shows Attended: 40+

Favorite Experience: Lemonwheel and NYE 2000

Origin of recipe: Drunk tailgate leftovers

Favorite memory of sharing recipe: People finding out they taste better than they sound

Song this recipe is: "Big Black Furry Creatures from Mars"

Jalapeño Cheddar Crunch Dogs

Ingredients:
Hot dogs
Jalapeños
Cheddar cheese
Fritos

Directions:
1. Grill hot dogs to order.
2. Top with jalapeños, Fritos and cheddar cheese.
3. Place on bun.
4. Stuff your face.

Serves: 8

Snacks

Name: Parker Harrington

Location: Boston, MA

Occupation: Real Estate Manager

Shows Attended: 200+

Favorite Song: "You Enjoy Myself"

Favorite Experience: Amy's Farm. Great crowd, low key, cap to a fun summer and an interesting time in Phishstory.

Origin of recipe: Heard about car-engine cooking on the radio and started making wings.

Favorite memory of sharing recipe: Everyone who eats them the first time is shocked about how they were cooked.

Song this recipe is: "Gotta Jiboo!"

Show this recipe is: Woodstock, Third Ball. As that show was, these wings are a total surprise!

Under the Harry Hood Wings

Ingredients:
36 chicken wings
1 bottle ketchup
1 cup red wine vinegar
1 tablespoon red pepper flakes
1 cup minced jalapeños
6 cloves garlic
3 tablespoons honey
1 tablespoon brown sugar
Sprinkle of salt
1 teaspoon black pepper
Splash of Tabasco sauce
Splash of Worcestershire sauce

Directions:
Mix together all ingredients and pour over chicken wings. Cover tightly in the fridge for at least 24 hours before road tripping or pack them in your cooler. Drain wings (save the marinade) and divide into three foil packages of 12 wings each. Brush with marinade, then triple-wrap each package tightly. Make sure the packages are tight and that nothing is leaking! About four hours before hitting the lot on the road trip, place the packages in a medium-hot part of car engine and make sure they're not interfering with anything. Close (Harry) hood and drive about 250 miles or four hours, depending on traffic. (Ok, so getting into IT, Coventry, or Clifford Ball it would have only been three miles). Get to lot. Unpack. Pop hood. Unwrap packages and you have tasty, tasty, wings ready to enjoy!

Serves: 6

Snacks

Name: Kate Zonis

Location: NYC

Occupation: Artist & healthfoods chef

Shows Attended: 30 or so

Favorite Song: "Bathtub Gin," "Reba," "Silence in the Morning" (plus the others I've mentioned in the previous recipe)

Origin of recipe: made it up!

Favorite memory of sharing recipe: I perfected this recipe while living in Portland, Oregon. My memories of this involved using amazing, locally made ingredients and friends' vegetables. This was an amazing dish to eat on a drizzly, dim Oregon night.

Song this recipe is: "If I Could" (because people didn't know how to make tempeh, but now they will)

Show this recipe is: Let's see…last set, second night, at Festival 8, Halloween. That shit was funky and I got to dance next to the most amazing costumed freaks. It was a warm night full of good energy, as the tempeh dish is a warm meal full of good energy. (Okay, it's a stretch, but both good things!)

Let's go Out to Dinner and Eat Some Tempeh

Ingredients:
12 ounces tempeh (any kind will do)
⅓ cup soy sauce
½ cup water
⅓ cup olive oil
¼ cup agave nectar
2 inches fresh ginger
1 whole garlic clove
One or two bunches of dark leafy greens such as kale, collards, or swiss chard
Garlic
Tablespoon olive oil
Dash of water
¾ cup quinoa
1 ¼ cups water

Directions:

1. Cut tempeh into "finger" sized pieces about ½ inch thick by 4 inches long. Chop ginger and garlic really small, or throw all ingredients into a blender. Put tempeh on baking sheet that's been oiled or that has parchment paper on it. Combine them all and pour ¾ of the mixture over the tempeh. Halfway through baking, put the last ¼ of the mixture over tempeh.
2. While tempeh is baking, boil water for quinoa and add quinoa when it's reached a light boil. Boil for about 20 minutes, or until your water is absorbed and you can no longer see the little dot in the middle of each grain.
3. Meanwhile, rip or cut up greens and mince garlic. Sauté garlic over a low flame with olive oil for a minute or two. Quickly add a dash of water and salt. Don't overcook. Literally, 30 seconds will do.

Serve all together.
Serves: 3

Salads

Name: Concert Creations

Location: Queens, NY

Occupation: Optician/Artist

Shows Attended: 0

Favorite Song: "I Awoke"

Favorite Experience: Working with Pete on this website

Origin of recipe: Family recipe

Favorite memory of sharing recipe: We take it on the road to cut expenses at the food stands.

Song this recipe is: "I Awoke"

Show this recipe is: The tuna bounces through the pasta.

Shells-n-Fish Salad

Ingredients:
1 pound Barilla medium shells
¾ cup Hellman's mayonnaise
2 hardboiled eggs
½ teaspoon black pepper
½ teaspoon Lawry's seasoned salt
1 tablespoon dried minced onion
½ teaspoon dill pickle juice
2 cans tuna Phish

Directions:

1. Boil pasta, let cool.
2. Hard-boil 2 eggs, let cool and peel.
3. In a large sealable tupperware bowl, add pasta, sliced eggs, mayo, pepper, seasoned salt, onion, pickle juice, and tuna.
4. Stir all ingredients and chill before serving.

Serves: 4

Salads

Name: Lauren Ann

Location: New Jersey

Occupation: Designer/Yoga Instructor/Health Counselor

Shows Attended: 19

Favorite Song: "Weekapaug Groove"!

Favorite Experience: I love looking out at the crowd during shows (especially in arenas where you can see more of it) and watching it move like waves. We all get lost in our own flow from the music, creating this gorgeous, pulsing energy together…it's such a beautiful, powerful thing to experience and to be a part of!!!

Origin of recipe: I was in my kitchen last weekend, and wasn't sure what to make, so I got creative and used what I had available! It's SO yummy!

Favorite memory of sharing recipe: Watching my friend's face as he enjoyed the sweetness, crunchiness, nuttiness, bitterness and freshness all in one bite!!!

Song this recipe is: "Talk"

Show this recipe is: 11/13/97, Thomas & Mack Center, Las Vegas, NV…one of my FAVORITE shows!!! It's got the perfect array of songs that flow together so

well, kinda like all of the flavors in this salad!

Slave To The Colorful Quinoa Salad!

Ingredients:
I am not very exact with my measurements, so if you have to add more or less of something please go ahead and do so to your liking. I like to approach my cooking as I do with my art…I get out all my supplies, PLAY, and see what happens!
1 cup quinoa (after cooking it makes about 3 cups; you may not need all of the quinoa for this recipe and can save the rest for something else)
½ block firm tofu (optional)
½ red pepper
½ green pepper
½ yellow pepper
½ orange pepper
½ orange (you can also squeeze fresh lime/lemon into salad if you don't have oranges)
½ red onion
2 handfuls raw, unsalted cashews
Handful dried cranberries
Cilantro to taste (optional)
Mint to taste (optional)
2 tablespoons dijon mustard
A few splashes orange juice
1 tablespoon olive oil

Directions:
Cook quinoa and let cool. Chop peppers, onion and orange into tiny pieces. Drain tofu block and cut into bite-size pieces. Mix mustard, olive oil, orange juice in a large bowl, adding quinoa, chopped peppers, onion, orange and tofu. Add chopped, fresh cilantro and/or mint if you have them on hand. Take a handful or two of cashews, crunch with your fist, and add to the mix. Throw in dried cranberries and mix well. Add sea salt and/or a squeeze of lemon to taste. So yummy! ENJOY!!!!!!

Serves: 3

Salads

Name: Jason Cervantes

Location: Los Angeles, CA

Occupation: Selling steaks & martinis (waiter)

Shows Attended: 17

Favorite Song: Usually the one situated in the middle of the set.

Favorite Experience: Meeting Gordo in Los Angeles when he was here doing a voice-over for The Simpsons (2001-ish). I followed him to the bathroom, peed in a stall next to him. Pretended not to know who he was but told him he "looked very familiar"(while we were peeing), asking him if he had "been on TV before?" He said "Yeah. I've been on David Letterman." I said "Sweet." Then I bought him a Bass ale, handed it to him and proceeded to profess my love for him and the band. He ended up coming back to our house, jammed with us (he on my banjo, I on guitar) then I took him back to his hotel, The Portofino in Redondo Beach, CA. My most amazing Phish experience, which is more of a Mike Gordon from Phish experience. Thanks for letting me share.

Origin of recipe: I work in restaurants. I plagarized.. except for the name. That's all me…kind of.

Favorite memory of sharing recipe: Thanksgiving last year.

Song this recipe is: This salad is the "YEM" vocal jam.

Show this recipe is: It'd be a Halloween set (not big enough to be a whole show) because of its identity issues. It kind of wants to be a dessert.

My Sweet Salad

Ingredients:
Amounts of each may vary depending on personal preferences and servings and sizes and appetites and emotions and allergies and strengths and weaknesses and I'm spent.

Mixed greens.
Maple vinaigrette (or any sweet vinaigrette)
Crumbled bleu cheese (goat cheese MIGHT work)
Pecans (candied if possible, but any nuts will work)
Sliced pears (or apples or dried cranberries or any other salad-able fruit)

Directions:
1. Toss and enjoy…yourself.

Serves: 1

Salads

Name: Julie Parker

Location: Germany, Florida, Texas, Indiana

Occupation: Web Content Analyst

Shows Attended: 95 (As of Summer 2010)

Favorite Song: "First Tube"

Favorite Experience: Wow, there are so many, we'll go with my second favorite. 2/15/03, Vegas. After the show we hopped on the 'Clint Holmes' and we were packed in there like sardines! Then the radio broke out the Black Crowes' "Hard to Handle" and we all sang along all the way to the hotel.

Origin of recipe: My company just LOVES to have carry-ins, but of course, they don't typically give us much notice. So, this is one of those "Hmmmm, what do I have in my pantry and fridge that I could throw together and make something delicious with?" recipes that actually DID turn into something delicious.

Favorite memory of sharing recipe: I took it in to the work carry-in and everyone raved about it.

Song this recipe is: "Party Time"

Show this recipe is: 3/1/03 Greensboro. My friend and I weren't even going to go to this show, and by a bunch of happy accidents, we ended up with tickets and we booked the flight and went and it was one of the most fun shows that run! This recipe was a "happy accident" that turned out great!

Party Time Pasta Salad

Ingredients:
1 red onion
1 red bell pepper
1 yellow bell pepper
1 orange bell pepper
2 packages grape tomatoes
1 small can green olives
1 large can black olives
Two 8-ounce packages cubed cheese
1 large package pepperoni
1 small summer sausage
Half a box cooked spiral pasta
1 bottle Italian dressing
1 package Italian seasoning

Directions:

1. Cook the pasta and drain.
2. Chop up the peppers and onion and half the tomatoes and olives.
3. Mix in a bowl with dried Italian seasoning.
4. Halve the pepperoni and slice and quarter the sausage.
5. Add meats and cheese cubes to mixture *see note below in step 6 before adding cheese cubes!
6. Pour Italian dressing (quantity to taste) and mix it all together.
7. Chill for several hours or overnight (if leaving overnight, wait to add the cheese cubes until just before serving so they don't get mushy from the dressing).
8. Pour on a little more dressing right before serving (quantity to taste) and mix.

Serve chilled.

Serves: 12-20 depending on portion size.

Salads

Name: Sharon

Location: Buffalo, NY

Occupation: Office Manager

Shows Attended: More than 20

Origin of recipe: My mother-in-law used to make this for my husband when he was younger, before he met me and now I carry it on. It is only made when returning from a tour or show.

Favorite memory of sharing recipe: Every time we eat it.

Dead Salad

Ingredients:
Pasta
Italian dressing or other marinade
And whatever you have to put in it:
Mushrooms
Green peppers
Olives
Cheese
Leftovers

Directions:
1. Make pasta.
2. Cut up everthing else.
3. Mix everything together.
4. Chill.
5. Add Italian dressing or marinade when you're ready to eat.

Serves: 4

Salads

Name: Lee Crumpton

Location: North Carolina

Occupation: Professional Music Freek

Shows Attended: About 50

Favorite Song: "Maze"

Favorite Experience: My first show was a lifechanging event, The Boathouse, Norfolk, 1992. The music of Phish and similar bands lead me to form The Home Grown Music Network in 1995. Visit us online at www.HomeGrownMusic.net and discover your next favorite band!

Origin of recipe: I've been making it for years for the crew that works our vending booth at music festivals. For just a few bucks this will provide a hot, hearty meal for lots of hungry hippies.

Favorite memory of sharing recipe: I always make extra and share with my neighboring vendors. They love it and they don't have to leave their booth to go buy expensive festival food.

Song this recipe is: "You Enjoy Myself"

Lee's Festie Pasta

Ingredients:
Base: Knorr (formerly Lipton) Cheddar Broccoli pasta mix. Use 1 pack for every 2 to 3 people you want to feed. I usually make 3 packs at a time and that will feed 6 to 9 folks. The ingredients below are based on 3 packs. This dish allows for much improvisation, so you can throw in whatever you have available.
Optional ingredients:
FESTIVAL version (stuff that will keep without refrigeration)
1 can mixed veggies
1 can black or kidney beans
1 large can tuna
1 jar medium salsa
Cheez-Its or Goldfish or chips for added texture
HOME version
Fresh veggies from garden or fridge (broccoli, peas, tomatoes, peppers, carrots, beans, cauliflower, cooked potatoes
1 can black or kidney beans
Chopped boneless cooked chicken (optional)
1 jar medium salsa
Chips
Spices (improvise with what you have, some like it hot)
Grated cheddar or pepper jack cheese
Butter or margarine (optional)

Directions:
1. Follow directions on package for adding water and butter (optional). If making multiple packs at once, reduce the amount of water required. You can always add a bit more if/when needed. If you end up with too much water, you can add extra chips to help soak it up.
2. Bring water/butter to boil and add pasta mix, veggies, cheese, spices, meat etc. Cook till pasta is done and add salsa. Stir.
3. Garnish with chips.

Serves: 8

Salads

Name: Kate Zonis

Location: NYC

Occupation: Artist & healthfoods chef

Shows Attended: 30 or so

Favorite Song: "Harry Hood"

Origin of recipe: I made it up I just tried to take all sorts of super-healthy things and make 'em taste yummy.

Favorite memory of sharing recipe: This meal is literally just the opposite of a "Down with Disease" situation. The salad is undeniably one of the healthiest things a person could eat. As a personal chef, I specialize in cooking for people with disease and/or food allergies. This recipe is free of allergens, and contains many life-force super foods. Regardless of with whom I share this, it's great knowing they're getting all that amazing nutrition.

Song this recipe is: "Down with Disease"

Show this recipe is: Keyspan Park in Brooklyn, second night. A diverse crowd, hearty Brooklyn freaks. The real deal.

Sprouting in a Jar - Kale & Sprout Salad

Ingredients:
½ cup brown lentils for sprouting
½ gallon jar for sprouting (wide-mouthed mason jars are great)
Cheesecloth or thin cloth or jar screen
One head of organic kale (I like lacinato)

Marinade:
Juice and pulp of two lemons
1 pinch fresh ginger
1 whole bulb garlic
2 tablespoons Braggs amino acids (add more if you like saltiness) OR
2 tablespoons nama shoyu (really awesome raw soy sauce) if you can eat wheat
1 teaspoon raw agave nectar
¼ cup unfiltered apple cider vinegar (I like Braggs)
⅓ cup flax seeds
⅓ cup crushed almonds and/or walnuts
⅓ cup nutritional yeast
⅓ cup hemp seeds
Whatever else you like adding to a salad

(*Recipe continued on page 51*)

Illustration: Cody Schibi

Sprouting in a Jar –
Kale & Sprout Salad (continued)

Directions:

1. Sprouting lentils takes two days. Soak lentils for about 8 hours. Then rinse and drain. Put them in a jar, and put cloth over lid with rubber band, making sure it's secure. Allow water to slowly drain off by placing it on an incline of about 45 degrees. Rinse and drain 2 to 3 times a day for two days. When sprouts get as long as the lentils themselves, put a lid on the jar and place in your fridge.
2. Rip and "massage" the kale to loosen its fibers. You don't need to go crazy with this, a quick fluffing will do.
3. Put marinade ingredients in blender and blend until it's a smooth liquid.
4. Massage the liquid over the kale, and add toppings. Toss it all together. Let it sit for anywhere from five minutes to an hour before eating. This salad keeps for about three days.

Note: if you think digesting raw kale will be hard on your tummy, think again. By massaging the kale and adding the lemon juice, you are very actively breaking down the roughage. This salad is amazingly easy to digest. If you understand the concept behind ceviche, the same principle applies.

Note 2: Sprouts are, in my opinion, the healthiest thing you can possibly eat!

Serves: 4

Sandwiches

Name: Fuzz and Carrie

Location: Connecticut

Occupation: Caravan of Thieves

Shows Attended: 5

Favorite Song: "Waste"

Favorite Experience: Big Cypress 2000

Origin of recipe: Variation on a recipe from a book called "How to Cook Everything Vegetarian"

Favorite memory of sharing recipe: Share? After you taste it, you won't want to share either.

Song this recipe is: "Meat"

Show this recipe is: All of them, it's nuts!

Rebirth Nut Burger (Vegetarian)

Ingredients:
1 medium onion
1 cup mixed nuts
1 cup raw rolled oats
2 tablespoons BBQ Sauce
1 teaspoon chili powder
Salt to taste
1 egg
2 tablespoons oil (grapeseed or corn)

Directions:
1. Grind the onion in a food processor. Add nuts and oats and pulse to chop but not too finely. Add the BBQ sauce, chili powder, salt, pepper and egg. Process briefly. You want the mixture to be moist but not loose.
2. Let the mixture rest for a few minutes then shape into 4 to 6 patties. Heat the oil in a large nonstick pan over medium heat. When the oil is hot, add the burgers. Cook for 5 minutes, then turn over. Lower the heat a bit and cook the other side for 3 to 4 minutes. This is the time to add cheese.
3. Serve on a bun with cheese (smoked Gouda, cheddar), lettuce, tomato, fried onions and BBQ sauce or serve on a plate with mashed potatoes, vegetables and mushroom gravy.

Serves: 4

Sandwiches

Name: Taraleigh Weathers

Location: Burlington, VT

Occupation: Magazine Maker and Holistic Health Counselor

Shows Attended: I'm not sure, but I've been to a lot!

Favorite Song: "Tela"

Favorite Experience: I've had many, but one of my favorites was at Big Cypress. After we danced for many hours to the sounds of Phish, the sun began to rise and they finished their sets. They played a recording of the Beatles' "Here Comes the Sun" and I was front center where I had been for hours, and everyone started singing along and hugging. It was beautiful.

Origin of recipe: I didn't know what to make for dinner and I saw a can of chickpeas and got creative.

Favorite memory of sharing recipe: I made these for some friends and they all loved them! I heard things like, "This is the best veggie burger I've ever had." "Can I please have the recipe?" "mmmmmmm"

Song this recipe is: "Run Like an Antelope because they are out of control."

Show this recipe is: It would be the Hampton run of 2009 because you didn't know what to expect and it ended up being awesome.

This is Not a Meat Stick It's a Chickpea Burger!

Ingredients:
1 can chickpeas, rinsed
1 cup textured vegetable protein, soaked in ¾ cup water
½ onion, chopped
2 cloves garlic, chopped
1 teaspoon chili powder
½ cup breadcrumbs
1 egg, beaten
Salt and pepper to taste

Directions:

1. Place chickpeas, textured vegetable protein, onion, garlic, and chili powder in a blender and blend.
2. Place all ingredients in a mixing bowl.
3. Add breadcrumbs, salt, pepper, and egg and mix.
4. Heat a frying pan coated with olive oil on medium heat.
5. Mold mixture into burger patties.
6. Fry for about 5 minutes on each side.

Serves: 6

Sandwiches

Name: Tim D.

Location: Indianapolis, IN

Occupation: Factory Boy

Shows Attended: 50?

Favorite Song: "Mango"

Favorite Experience: Saw them the first time, 6/19/95, Deer Creek, with my 12-year-old daughter. Hooked from the start. Mostly Midwest runs. I am a proud member of the Phellowship. From the lot to the encore, it's a spiritual journey.

Origin of recipe: Made it for my kids. It's just a sweet combo.

Favorite memory of sharing recipe: Selling them on our annual summer run.

Song this recipe is: "Fluffhead"

Show this recipe is: 6/19/2009, 14th anniversary of our first show. Sickest Fluffhead I've ever heard.

The Phluffhead

Ingredients:
1 loaf bread, your choice
1 jar peanut butter, your choice
1 jar marshmallow creme

Directions:
1. Spread peanut butter on one slice of bread.
2. Marshmallow creme on another.
3. Put together.
4. Repeat 10 times.
5. Put sandwiches back into bread sack.
6. Cruise the lot, sell, trade or eat them as you see fit.
7. Mainly have fun.

Serves: 10

Sandwiches

Name: Jeremy

Location: Royal Oak, MI

Occupation: Future chauffeur extraordinaire

Shows Attended: 60ish

Favorite Song: Can't name one, but currently digging on "Splinters of Hail"

Favorite Experience: 12/06/97 will always hold a special place with me. Second show, mind was blown, face was melted. Hampton '09 shows are up there with the most special and purely emotional experiences of my life. Fest 8 was beautiful, ragged perfection.

Origin of recipe: Stole and embellished/improved upon a 7 to 11 snackwrap I discovered last summer. The discovery resulted from too much laziness to go grocery shopping, and subsequently cured my problem because I started to get self-conscious about buying all they had (which was usually three of four) at once every day.

Favorite memory of sharing recipe: When people first bite in, and their immediate reaction is a look of slight confusion, then wondering surprise upon their faces, and they proceed to smile and nod while chewing–just like in a real–life commercial. Also, the rave reviews, using such descriptions as "mmm, so savory," "This is just really *quite* delightful" and "After eating your Delicious Fucking Sandwich, I went home and made love to my wife for the first time in seven years."

Song this recipe is: "Probably Fast Enough for You," as it is so smooth and tasty.

Show this recipe is: Big Cypress, because it's just that good.

Little Jimmy's Delicious Phucking Sandwich

Ingredients:
Naan Bread in any flavor. I prefer garlic. Also great with a spinach wrap, but I recommend the Naan all day long.
Hummus (any flavor will do, I love either garlic or roasted red pepper)
Handful of baby spinach
Handful of shredded carrots
Handful of broccoli slaw
A few slivered red onions
Several slices of red/yellow pepper
A bit of crumbled bleu cheese (crumbled goat cheese is also delicious but a little more mild)
Small handful of dried cranberries
One or two dollops of basalmic vinaigrette

Directions:
It's just a sandwich, so there's really not much to it.
Spread entire surface of bread or wrap with hummus, and pile on the veggies to your liking. Don't go too heavy on the cranberries or vinagrette, as they are there for subtle complexity, rounding out the dominating taste and texture of the vegetables and adding a little sweetness to the flavor of the hummus and the cheese. Then again, that's just me. Go crazy. Experiment. Add your own ingredients.* When you are satisfied that your creation is complete, fold, eat and achieve instant enlightenment as well as becoming irresistibly attractive to the opposite sex. Or the same sex, whatever. Nothin' wrong with that.

*DO NOT add sardines or any kind of nasty "snack fish" to the Delicious Sandwich. That would simply negate the whole point of it being "Delicious" instead of "Disgusting."

Serves: 1

Sandwiches

Name: Rye Palmer

Location: Portland, Oregon

Occupation: Musician

Shows Attended: 30 or so

Favorite Song: "Weekapaug Groove"

Favorite Experience: When Trey asked Chris to turn the lights out at the gorge in '97 during the Hood encore.

Origin of recipe: Revised it from an SAT question in grade school. Using bread instead of an English muffin.

Favorite memory of sharing recipe: We made them in a lot, somewhere, sometime. Everyone loved them. It was total chaos in the "kitchen." Ingredients everywhere, people in line were made to hold the flashlight. The rest of the details are a bit fuzzy… Hilarious, though.

Show this recipe is: Ashland, Oregon, April 3rd, 1991. I think this one because it's right around the time I came up with the recipe in a town 10 miles from my childhood home.

Mr. Palmer's Pizza Sandwich

Ingredients:
Two slices, bread, white, grain, wheat, potato, or flax.
Ragu Pizza Quick Sauce (or any other pizza sauce)
Mozzarella cheese (shredded)
Parmesan cheese
Garlic powder
Optional ingredients: pepperoni slices, feta cheese, one meatball, black olives, crushed red peppers, fresh basil, fresh oregano

Directions:
Make it like a grilled cheese.
Fairly simple recipe here.
Cook it in a medium frying pan on medium heat.

1. Butter one side of each piece of bread, place one in the pan and set the other aside.
2. Spread about 1 to 1½ tablespoons of pizza sauce on the bread in the pan.
3. Add a liberal amount of garlic powder on top of the sauce.
4. Add your cheese.
5. Add your meat if you're a carnivore.
6. Add any of the optional ingredients now.
7. Spread 1 to 1½ tablespoons of sauce to the bread you set aside in step 1.
8. Place that slice of bread on top and you're ready to go.
9. Cook both sides until golden brown.
10. Enjoy.

Serves: 1

Sandwiches

Name: Jake Cohen

Location: Grew up in Boston, live in New York

Occupation: Grad Student

Shows Attended: 61

Favorite Song: "Tela"

Favorite Experiences: Big Cypress; waiting in line for Roseland tickets in 2000; first time to the Gorge in 2003.

Origin of recipe: Every time I left a show, I was starving for some tasty non-vegetarian lot food. It's not that I don't like vegetarian, but sometimes after four hours of dancing your head off, you want a little more extra sustenance. So I decided to cater to the crowd that thought the same way I did. We sold hot sandwiches that we cooked on a griddle in the parking lot during the entire Summer 2003 tour. Our stand was called "Split Open and Melt" because we did melted sandwiches. I worked at a pizza restaurant that would caramelize big batches of onions for a topping, and I wanted to make a sandwich with them. One day I saw Sierra Nevada Pale Ale Honey Mustard at the grocery store, and the idea came to me. We named it after a song because we thought it would make people stop to see what was in it.

Favorite memory of sharing recipe: Cooking at the Gorge after the 7/12/03 show, we had a bright lantern at our stand right on one of the main paths, but a little bit off from Shakedown. Four guys with instruments asked if they could set up near our stand because of our light. They were a bluegrass band, and they played a full one-hour set of originals and covers, attracting a crowd of about 50.

Song this recipe is: "Guyute," of course! Or "Split Open and Melt".

Show this recipe is: 11/2/98, Salt Lake City, Utah. 10/31/98 was the popular choice, but it was the overlooked 11/2/98 that stole the show Halloween.

The Guyute Sandwich

Ingredients:

<u>For the onions:</u>
2 yellow onions
1 tablespoon sugar
½ teaspoon ground black pepper
Salt
Few drops vanilla extract
2 tablespoons extra virgin olive oil

<u>For the sandwich:</u>
Thin sliced black forest ham (as much or little as you like)
1 to 2 slices Swiss cheese
Sierra Nevada Pale Ale Honey Mustard (or any other high-quality brand of honey mustard)
Any kind of bread (recommendations: Portuguese, scali, wheat/multigrain, sourdough)
Butter

Directions:
For the onions: Peel and thinly slice onions. Heat olive oil over medium heat and add onions. Salt well and add sugar. Cook onions until translucent. Some browning is OK, but don't over-brown, adding oil if necessary. Once onions are slightly browned and very soft, turn heat down to low/medium-low and add pepper and drops of vanilla. Cook until onions have melted and have a brown consistency, 45 minutes minimum, stirring occasionally. Onions are best if given 1 to 2 hours cooking time. When done, let cool so onions can develop more color/flavor. This step can be done in large quantities up to a day or more before, and will keep for about 4 to 5 days in refrigerator.

(*Recipe continued on page 65*)

Sandwiches

weekend in 1998. The Guyute wasn't the most popular sandwich we sold, that honor goes to the Mexican Cousin, with turkey, bacon, cheddar, tomato, and chipotle mayo. But the Guyute was definitely the overlooked sandwich which, when chosen, was clearly the best.

The Guyute Sandwich (continued)

For the sandwich:
Spread butter liberally on bread and place on pre-heated griddle. Spread mustard on bread. Spread thin layer of caramelized onion on bread.
Meanwhile, place ham on griddle, then add Swiss cheese on top. Once cheese begins to sweat and melt after 1 minute, stack ham/cheese on top of one piece of bread, and then top with remaining slice of bread. Let cook for 1 or 2 more minutes on each side, until cheese is melty or bread is well-browned. Note: since Swiss cheese doesn't melt as well as some others, you can drop the slice of cheese directly onto the griddle for just a second before putting it on top of the ham. This will result in a meltier sandwich.
Enjoy with a Sierra Nevada Pale Ale and the Went Gin.

Serves: 1

Sandwiches

Name: Zach Hostetter

Location: Ames, IA

Occupation: Gas Station Clerk/Student

Shows Attended: 6

Favorite Song: "Tweezer"

Favorite Experience: I prefer to listen to shows on my headphones, so as to get the full audio experience. The best live feeling was the Julius at Alpine '03. It is a cliche, I know, but it just kept raging and raging to end the set.

Origin of recipe: Family fishing trips (shore lunch)

Favorite memory of sharing recipe: The ease in making it was enough to convince others to try it.

Song this recipe is: "Tube" (simple rock and roll at first, and then funk in your mouth!)

Show this recipe is: Summer '93 stuff, because it is a simple recipe, like those shows, but it has a special surprise, like most of those shows.

Onion Dog

Ingredients:
8 Hot dogs (I like Ball Park Franks)
Dry Lipton Onion Soup Mix
Butter
Buns

Directions:

1. Butterfly the dogs and pack them with the soup mix and some butter.
2. Grill them open-side-up until soup mix and butter melt together.
3. Butter the buns and toast them.
4. Serve the oniony-buttery delicious dogs on the toasted buns.

Serves: 8

Sandwiches

Name: Greg Gallina

Location: Erie, PA

Occupation: Financial Advisor

Shows Attended: 55

Favorite Song: "Reba"

Favorite Experiences: The first concert I went to, in 1994 in Erie, PA, was really an eye-opener. It was a beautiful day, a beautiful theater and a beautiful setlist. I remember looking at Trey's fingers during Sparkle and was amazed at how impossibly fast they were moving. The Reba was absolutely flawless; I still have not heard an equal to or better version to date. They closed with The Squirming Coil which was absolutely tremendous. They all walked off stage, one by one, leaving Page to play an absolutely breathtaking piano solo. The Funky Bitch encore was smoking hot. One of my all-time favorite shows.

Origin of recipe: When I was in grad school at NYU, my roommate and I were preparing food to sell at the Gathering of the Vibes, 2001. After trying many burritos on many different lots, I decided I could make a much better and more satisfying burrito. After drinking for several hours, at approximately 2 am, I chopped off part of my left thumb while cutting up green pepper. It was a strange sensation. It took about 3 seconds to

realize what happened. I looked at the tip of my thumb and it was missing. I could see the bone, and it took a second or two for the blood to start pouring out. My roommate, Mike Aspite, immediately went to the fridge and poured some milk over a glass of ice. He said he had been watching National Geographic Channel a couple of weeks ago and the best thing for a severed digit was to keep it on ice. So, I picked up the severed appendage and threw it in the milk. We wrapped my hand in paper towels and several minutes later we were in a cab on the way to the hospital. The cab driver turned around to ask where we were going, I was screaming HOSPITAL, my roommate Mike had part of my mutilated thumb in a glass of milk and I was bleeding profusely. The driver gunned it, dropped us off at Veteran's Hospital. We walked in and they would not admit me as a patient since I was not a veteran. They called

20+ Veggie Burritos Mussolini

Ingredients:
1 cup brown rice
6 cloves garlic, chopped
1 large white onion, chopped
1 large red onion, chopped
1 large green pepper, chopped
1 large red pepper, chopped
2 small red bliss potatoes, cut into ¼ inch cubes
½ okra, cut into ¼ inch slices
1 small container button mushrooms (You can substitute more exotic mushrooms if you so desire)
1 bag mixed frozen broccoli and cauliflower
1 bag mixed frozen peas, carrots, lima beans, green beans and corn
1 bag mixed frozen green and yellow squash
Two 8-ounce cans water chestnuts, chopped
16 ounce can black beans, drained
16 ounce can cannellini beans, drained
16 ounce can black-ryed peas, drained
3 tablespoons chili powder
1 tablespoon cayenne pepper (or less to taste)
½ tablespoon dried cumin
1 tablespoon dried basil
Salt and pepper, to taste
Extra virgin olive oil
20 to 30 large flour tortillas
* Fresh products can be substituted out for any of the frozen or canned products.

(*Recipe continued on page 71*)

me a cab to another hospital. At this point, I started to get worried that too much time had passed and they wouldn't be able to reconnect my thumb. When we arrived at the next hospital, they immediately took me in. It looked like someone had been murdered, with all the blood on my clothes. They actually had a Severed Digit Ward they admitted me to. Next thing I know, I'm on a gurney next to some Indian guy who had all the fingers on his right hand lopped off in some horrible "framing" incident. This guy took it like an absolute gentleman. He was even telling jokes to the doctor. I had never felt like such a pussy in my whole life. There was a guy who just chopped off all of his fingers and I was sitting there crying like a little girl over just the tip of one. It would be the first time I had some issues with just the tip, but thats a different story. Next, the doctor finally came to see me. He asked why on god's green earth did I have my thumb on milk. By this time, all the ice had melted and most of the liquid had spilled out. I said we saw it on TV. He had no idea what we were talking about. He fished the severed part of my thumb from the cup with a pair of medical tweezers. He paid me no mind and stated "we can't save this." He then threw it into the trash. At this point, I couldn't help but notice that the Indian guy next to me started screaming in pain, as they were washing his wounds with a saline solution. Simultaneously, the doctor pulled out a cauterizing pen and sealed my thumb up. It was pretty painful. He said the tip of my thumb would grow back and not to worry. When he dressed the wound, the thumb on my left hand looked like it had a mini chef hat on. On our way back to the apartment we stopped to do some celebratory shots of Jägermeister. Mike heard it first. "Hey dude, did your thumb just say something?". I replied, "I don't think so." We went back to the apartment, threw out the batch of burritos we were working on, pounded a few more beers, cleaned up and went to bed. The next day, I woke up and there was a little face drawn on my thumb. We had many burritos to make and started at about 10 am. It was at this point I heard the first demands from my thumb, he told me to start drinking heavily and the burrito making would go much quicker. My thumb also instructed me that instead of making several different batches, we should use all of the vegetables in one "mother" batch. Evil Chef Greg Jr., as he would later be named, had a direct vision for these burritos. Evil Chef Greg Jr. was soon making all the calls and dishing out heavy doses of insults to any who would listen. He even sprayed an innocent bystander in the eyes with Windex. But soon, the burritos would be done, they would be delicious and they would all be sold at The Gathering.

Favorite memory of sharing recipe: A hippie walked in eating another vendor's burrito. He liked our money-back guarantee, so he purchased a 20+ Veggie Burritos Mussolini. He took one bite then stated, "No more of these schwag-ass burritos for me!" and threw his previous, half-eaten burrito on the ground and walked away. It made me proud.

Song this recipe is: "BBFCFM"

Show this recipe is: The recipe was developed during a pretty intense period of my life. It was developed during some highly chaotic binge-drinking episodes, which are reminiscent of some of the highly chaotic sections of Big Black Furry Creatures From Mars. Especially when Fishman starts screaming gibberish.

20+ Veggie Burritos Mussolini

(continued)

Directions:
1. Drink 13 beers.
2. Prepare all ingredients ahead of time. Mix all frozen vegetables together in a large bowl. Prepare rice according to recipe on package. Set aside.
3. Cover the bottom of a large stock pot with EVOO (about ¼ inch) and cook over high heat. When the oil is hot, add garlic. Stir for 2 to 3 minutes.
4. Add chopped onions and cook over high heat for 7 minutes, constantly stirring.
5. Add half of the chili powder to the mixture. Stir vigorously.
6. Add green and red peppers and potato to the mixture.
7. Add ALL of the seasonings to the mixture. Allow to cook for 3 to 5 minutes, while gently stirring to prevent sticking.
8. Add okra and mushrooms.
9. Over the course of the next 10 to 15 minutes, slowly introduce ALL frozen vegetables into the mixture, stirring the whole time.
10. Once everything is warmed through, add water chestnuts and black and white beans. Cook for 5 to 7 minutes, gently stirring.
11. Add black-eyed peas to the mixture. If watery, stir vigorously over high heat to remove excess moisture.
12. Season with salt and pepper to taste. Add more of the other spices if you need to. The mixture should look thick and gooey. Some of the vegetables should have broken down by this point. If they haven't, keep cooking.
13. Remove mixture from heat. Blend in the brown rice that you have set aside. This mixture is the finished product. Taste to make sure the mixture is both delicious and tremendous.
14. With a large spoon, scoop the mixture onto the wraps and roll into a burrito form. Directions for this are usually on the back of the package.
15. Wrap in tin foil if you want to sell them at shows.
**Total cooking time should be about 45 minutes to 1 hour over high heat, depending on your stove.

Serves: 20

Sandwiches

Name: Joy Rose

Location: New Jersey

Occupation: Teacher

Shows Attended: About 25

Favorite Song: "Reba"

Favorite Experience: It's changed over the years. At first it was getting to the lot and finding my goodies for the night and then boogeying down. Now there are less goodies but still a lot of boogeying down. Now I like to bring my hula hoop and hoop my way through a set way in the back. Basically, the best is that moment at a show when you're giving the dancing everything you have, and you look around and realize everyone else is giving everything they have, too.

Origin of recipe: Basically, this one was born, like most things, from necessity. It was getting close to show time, and I had no ticket and only $20 going into the show. This was probably Garden State Arts Center (now PNC Bank - blech) in summer of '99. Good thing I had enough gas in my car to get to the lot. But anyway, I went to the store with $20, bought the ingredients, made the burritos at home, sold them in the lot before the show, was able to buy my ticket, eat vegetarian, and have a great show. What more can a girl ask for?

Favorite memory of sharing recipe: Seeing people after the show who bought a burrito before the show. They would say, "There's that chick with the great burritos! That did me RIGHT!" Stuff like that!

Song this recipe is: "Reba's Creation" - the finest in the nation!

Show this recipe is: 12/28/98 MSG, Hallelujah, I saw the light!

Cheap and Easy Vegan Burrito

Ingredients:
This is for a small "head stash" batch of burritos.
1 teaspoon olive oil
2 peppers (1 yellow, 1 green)
1 small onion
1 clove garlic
1 can vegetarian refried beans (the best are from Trader Joe's)
1 cup white basmati rice
2 medium tomatoes (tomatoes on the vine are best)
1 tablespoon butter (vegan butter possible)
Package of tortillas
You should be able to buy this at any grocery store for less than $20.

Directions:
1. Chop peppers, dice onions, mince garlic.
2. Heat olive oil on medium high heat until water sizzles on it.
3. Throw on garlic and onion and sauté until they turn slightly brown (but not too brown).
4. Add peppers and sauté until the onions are transparent. Keep at medium heat or else the garlic will burn.
5. In a separate pot, boil 2 cups of water for the rice. Add rice, set to low heat, cover, and cook for 16 minutes. After 16 minutes, remove from heat, fluff with fork, add butter and let sit.
6. Add refried beans to the rice, mixing well and heating on low.
7. Chop tomatoes. If any tomato juices run out while you are chopping, add that to the rice/beans mixture and stir.
8. Heat the tortillas on the range top for a few seconds on each side. Load on the rice/beans, then top with the sauté d veggies, then with tomatoes. Wrap burrito in foil. Should make about 6 hearty vegan burritos. If you make them in the early afternoon and nestle them together in an insulated bag, they will still be warm by lot time! Then you can say, "Warm vegan burritos!" while walking around and they will be gone in no time. Don't forget to save yourself one for after the show!

Serves: 6

Sandwiches

Name: Josh Mele

Location: Jacksonville, Fl

Occupation: Student/self-employed

Shows Attended: Not sure, but well over a hundred

Favorite Song: "Got Stuck Here"

Favorite Experience: The Spiritual combination of music, Phellowship & Recovery.

Origin of recipe: Some tour kid in a far off land, a long time ago…

Favorite memory of sharing recipe: That of obtaining enough gas money to get to the next show.

Song this recipe is: "Split Open and Melt"

Show this recipe is: Fall 2000 at shoreline, when Bob Weir came out and played a three-song encore with them. Good and cheesy.

The Sexy Garlic Grilled Cheese

Ingredients:
Two slices of the cheapest white bread available
Two slices of the cheapest American pasteurized processed cheese food singles
Vegetable oil spread (or the cheapest imitation butter product available)
Garlic powder (try to spend as little money as possible on this as well)

Directions:
1. Spread a light amount of butter product evenly on one side of each piece of bread. Be sure not to put too much on it, or it will make for a soggy sandwich.
2. Tear one piece of cheese in half and place on the unbuttered side of one of the pieces of bread. Place on outer edges with a gap in the center, and then place the other piece in the center so the cheese will be evenly distributed throughout the sandwich. Put the other piece of bread on the sandwich, buttered side out.
3. Sprinkle with garlic powder and place on pan.
4. After placing in pan, brown evenly on both sides. Make sure the heat is kind of low. This way the cheese will melt good and the bread won't burn.
5. You can wrap them up in aluminum foil and place 'em in a hot carrying bag for sales on the go, or cook 'em to order singing, "Sexy Garlic Grilled Cheese! WTF, it's only a buck!" (one dollar is suggested retail, but prices may vary.)

Serves: 1

Sandwiches

Name: Chad

Location: Baltimore, MD

Occupation: Shipping/recieveing

Shows Attended: 40

Favorite Song: "Golgi Apparatus"

Favorite Experience: Meeting Gordo in the parking lot in Camden, NJ on the 1999, Summer Tour…chit chat on his golf cart for a minute…then we turned around and scouted a parking lot band jammin' out….The bass player of the band was playing a upright electric bass and Mike came up out of the blue and did a little bass solo for the selected phans there and played "Kiss Is Just a Kiss"…great stuff…

Origin of recipe: This was a burrito I encountered in Virginia Beach in 1998 after the show. I saw the burrito slingers by our car in the parking lot with a life-size cut-out of Lionel Richie from his heyday in the '80s with the pink vest. The burritos had a great endorser, and the burrito itself was excellent.

Favorite memory of sharing recipe: Eating the burrito next to the life-sized Lionel Richie cut-out, I felt like he was there sharing the burrito experience with me and he was singing to me "Dancing on the Ceiling" in the background of my mind.

Song this recipe is: "Twist"

Show this recipe is: Philly '97, funky flavors coming from that burrito…just as those two-show stint at the Spectrum during Fall tour that year.

Lionel Richie Veggie Burritos

Ingredients:
Flavored flour tortilla (for example spinach)
Fresh avacados
Black beans
Cilantro
Pico de gallo
Sour cream
Black olives
Yellow onions
Jalenpeños
Lettuce
Hot sauce (bottle to leave on the vendor table as an option)

Directions:
Take two cans of black beans; drain and smash up the black beans. Take a saucepan and a camper stove top and heat the burner to a medium setting. Add the smashed black beans into the saucepan. Add diced yellow onions, fresh chopped jalenpeños, pico de gallo, and cilantro to the beans. Put the setting of the camper stove at a low-medium temp.
Once the beans are simmered and cooked, take your flour tortilla and your fixin' of shredded iceberg lettuce, black olives, and sour cream, Put the fixings in the middle of the flour tortilla (an amount able to be rolled up), make sure you have room to pour the cooked black beans in the wrap with the fixings. Once all is on the wrap take a piece a tin foil (twice the width of the flour tortilla) and carefully put the unwrapped burrito on the foil and do the wrap thing two (opposite sides of the widest part of the tortilla in with the bottom part the flour tortilla crease inward) then wrap that Lionel Burrito a bit tight in the foil….And serve it up like, "You're rolling in the Night"

Serves: 1

Sandwiches

Name: Michael Zwaryczuk

Location: Long Island, NY

Occupation: Project Manager

Shows Attended: Not enough

Favorite Song: "Antelope"

Favorite Experience: Besides the birth of my children and my wedding day, nothing will beat Big Cypress

Origin of recipe: This actually hasn't come about just yet but it is about to.

Favorite memory of sharing recipe: I can picture it invading the lots… no, not Shakedown… it'll be low-key and I'm not looking to make a buck, just want to share it in the mood.

Song this recipe is: "Mexican Cousin" segue into "Tela" (MCSIT)

Show this recipe is: The show hasn't happened yet but when it does it'll be the first meal my family and I have in the lots… regardless of whether we are camping or simply chillin' in the lot.

Mexican Cousin into Tela

Ingredients:
1 fajita wrap
Yellow rice
Monterey Jack cheese
Grilled chicken
* Hot sauce optional

Directions:
1. Place ingredients in a fajita wrap (hot or cold).
2. Roll it up.
3. Enjoy.

Serve hot or cold.

Serves: 1

Sandwiches

Name: Dave Smith

Location: Granby, CT

Occupation: Office Manager

Shows Attended: 15

Favorite Song: "David Bowie"

Favorite Experience: The last one. :-)

Origin of recipe: Family recipe

Song this recipe is: "Golgi Apparatus"

Grilled Peanut Butter Sandwich

Ingredients:
Jar of peanut butter
Loaf of bread (not too scrunched)
Butter or oil

Directions:
1. Spread peanut butter on one piece of bread and put another slice on top to make a sandwich.
2. Butter the outsides and cook on skillet till golden brown.
3. Flip and do same to other side.

You can substitute cheese (Cheez Whiz works great) for the grilled cheese lovers.

Serves: 9

Sandwiches

Name: Adam Lebin & Malaika Marion

Location: Chicago, IL. The Brown Sack Soup, Sandwich & Shake Shack

Occupation: Restaurant Owners

Shows Attended: 90 Plus

Favorite Song: "Col Forbin's Ascent"

Favorite Experience: Jazzfest in New Orleans in 1996 when the rain seemed to dissappear as Phish started playing.

Origin of recipe: Served at our restaurant The Brown Sack Soup, Sandwich & Shake Shack in the Logan Square neighborhood of Chicago

Favorite memory of sharing recipe: When my mom had the sandwich for the first time and her amazement at how something so Simple could be so good. Just like a great Phish jam.

Song this recipe is: "Simple"

Show this recipe is: The 1994 Halloween show where Simple was taken to new heights. The grilled veggie sandwich catches all our customers by surprise just like the epic version of Simple from Glen Falls, NY did.

The Simple Grilled Veggie Sandwich

Ingredients:
1 large plantain
Black beans
1 white onion
4 regular mushrooms
Vegetable oil
Cajun seasoning
Romaine lettuce
1 tomato
1 red onion
Spicey Dijon mustard
Italian seasoning
Marble rye bread
Provolone cheese

Directions:

1. Slice 1 large plantain horizontally. Slice ½ white onion. Slice 3 to 4 mushrooms.
2. Drain and wash 4 tablespoons of black beans.
3. Take one head of romaine lettuce. Slice into two halves, then slice part of one half into small strips. Slice ½ of a tomato. Slice ½ of a red onion.
4. Toast rye bread in toaster or toaster oven.
5. In a small sauté pan heat 1 tablespoon of vegetable oil.
6. Add plantains. Flip plantains once first side begins to brown.
7. Add handful of white onion, and handful of mushrooms.
8. Add black beans and dust all ingredients with cajun seasoning. Let sauté until plantains are browned on both sides. About 2 to 3 minutes on medium-hight heat.
Once this is accomplished add provolone cheese and cover with lid for 30 to 45 seconds.
9. Slide ingredients onto bread with spatula.
10. Top with shredded romaine. Top with 3 ½ slices of tomato. Top with a few slices of red onion. Add Dijon mustard to top slice of bread. Dust sandwich with Italian seasoning.
Cut in half and enjoy!

Serves: 1

Sandwiches

Name: Nessim Watson

Location: Western Massachusettes

Occupation: Foole

Shows Attended: Over 100…

Favorite Song: "Mike's Groove"

Favorite Experience: My first show, 2/17/90, blindly following my new girlfriend Peach to UMass from Hampshire College. $5 tickets scissor-cut from construction paper, a tiny room, and about 100 people. 'Nuff said. Widespread Panic opened. Phish started with Possum and I was hooked before the song ended. Hooked on the girl too. I married her. Say hi to us at the NE shows!

Origin of recipe: Dude, it's 6 pm and the stage is way across the festival grounds! What's quick and in the cooler?

Favorite memory of sharing recipe: Can't talk… eating.

Song this recipe is: See included setlist translation.

Show this recipe is: Some show in the future at the Gorge in Washington with the jagged cliffs and inspiring views. The setlist is a set one for sure. Col. Forbin into Secret Smile into fly Famous Mockingbird into Scents and Subtle Sounds into Col. Forbin. A date coming soon?

Colonel Forbin's A-Scent Setlist Sandwich

Ingredients:
English muffins
Cheese
Chicken Breast
Basil

Directions:
1. Prepare the Mockingbird in advance. (When you start a Forbin, you know it's coming, right?)
2. Cook chicken breast at home and store in reusable container. Place in cooler.
After proper preparation of kind herbs and cooks at campsite:
3. Fire up the propane stove under a frying pan.
4. Butter two halves of Forbin English muffin and fry one of them face down.
5. Once the sacred creed becomes yours to seize, devour and obey, flip the English muffin half as the unfinished Forbin then arpeggios into a healthy slice of Secret Smile cheese on top. Pick whatever kind of cheese you like. In some ways, they are all the same. ;-)
6. When the cheese has run its course on the muffin, it's *clearly* time for the Mockingbird.
7. Place cooked chicken breast in pan to warm it up.
8. Sprinkle Scents & Subtle Sounds directly onto the Secret Smile and place the Mockingbird on top.
9. Fry and add that second English muffin half.
10. Hand it to your friend.
*For setlist purists, who have never seen a Forbin return to Forbin, this can be made as an open-faced sandwich. Just sprinkle the Basil (S&SS) directly onto the cheese (Secret Smile), and then complete with the chicken breast (Mockingbird).

Serves: 1

Breakfast

Name: Scott and Aimee Decker

Location: Hoosick Falls, NY

Occupation:
Scott: Engineer
Aimee: Mom

Shows Attended: 250+ Combined

Favorite Song:
Scott: "Manteca"
Aimee: "Tweezer"

Favorite Experience: Probably Big Cypress, however it's hard to pick a favorite. We did get married in Vegas before the show on 2/16/03 so that was special.

Origin of recipe: Developed it from a favorite sandwich at a restaurant in Atlanta.

Favorite memory of sharing recipe: Don't really have one…

Song this recipe is: "Guy Forget"

Show this recipe is: It would be a Sunday night show following a weekend in Vegas. More of a first set to just satisfy your appetite after a long tiring weekend. Maybe a 10/1/2000 because this is kind of like a sandwich you have never met that you could not forget, its

name is Guy Forget…

Fried Egg "Sand-Wedge"

Ingredients:
1 egg
½ teaspoon butter
Veggie or real bacon (tempeh strips were our favorite)
Avocado slices
Vegenaise® (or mayo as substitute)
Lettuce
Tomato slices
2 slices of your favorite bread, English muffin, or bagel, toasted

Directions:
1. In a small skillet, melt butter over medium-high heat. Crack egg in pan (break the yolk), add salt and pepper to taste and cook to desired firmness.
2. Cook bacon according to directions.
3. Spread Vegenaise and place lettuce on a slice of bread. Place fried egg on top of the lettuce and then add bacon and tomato slices over the egg.
4. Spread Vegenaise on remaining slice of bread and add avocado slices.
5. Place on top of other half.
6. Cut Sand-Wedge in half and serve warm.

Add ketchup if desired.

Serves: 1

Breakfast

Name: Pete Mason

Location: Albany, NY

Occupation: Teacher

Shows Attended: 75 as of August 2010

Favorite Song: "Meatstick"

Favorite Experience: Big Cypress—I went down with my friends Chris and Kate, had the greatest time of our lives. Phish played. They were good, too.

Origin of recipe: The urge to make the greasiest breakfast possible, as it is a great hangover cure, and at the same time, the most unhealthy breakfast meal to eat. Vegans may want to stop reading now, for their own good.

Favorite memory of sharing recipe: Having some friends watch the process of making it, then enjoying it and having the expected reaction: "My God, I feel like I'm going to have a heart attack!" SUCCESS!!!

Song this recipe is: "Beauty of a Broken Heart"

Show this recipe is: 10/10/99 sloppy, delicious and unfinished this one is tough to eat all of.

The Coronary: Not For the Faint of Heart

Ingredients:
2 eggs
2 strips bacon
2 links sausage
1 chunk green pepper, diced
½ small white onion, diced
1 slice cheese (any kind)
2 slices rye bread (toasted)
1 small red potato
Olive oil
Salt and pepper

Directions:
1. Dice and boil the potato until it is firm but a fork can slightly break it apart. Then cook the potato in olive oil until brown. Remove, set off to side.
2. In the same pan with the same oil, cook the bacon and sausage to your liking. KEY - RETAIN THE GREASE!!!!
3. Then, cook the peppers and onions. Leaving them in the grease, crack two eggs and mix them around, forming an egg/onion/pepper combo that will fit on the rye toast.
4. You should toast the bread about this time.
5. Once the egg is getting near being done, put the sausage links on top, then the bacon strips, and the cheese until fully melted. Garnish with salt and pepper.
6. Put on bread, serve, and enjoy!
(This is NOT for those with heart conditions, the elderly, n00bs, or people from Nebraska.)

Breakfast

Name: Mike Jones

Location: NY

Shows Attended: A bunch

Favorite Song: Too many

Origin of recipe: Jebus told me about it.

Favorite memory of sharing recipe: The satisfying feeling after you eat this bad boy.

Song this recipe is: "Split Open and Melt"

Sweet Bacon Breakfast David Burrito

Ingredients:
3 eggs
½ sweet potato
2 strips of bacon
Brown sugar
Tortilla
Shredded cheddar/mexican cheese
Olive oil
Some spices (pepper, salt, garlic)

Directions:

1. Preheat oven to 425 degrees.
2. Grab a cookie sheet cover it with aluminum foil.
3. Put as many strips of bacon as you want to cook.
4. Sprinkle bacon with brown sugar.
5. Put in oven, cook for 4 to 5 mins then turn tray 180 degrees and cook for another 4 to 5 mins. 2 pieces of bacon is probably enough for the burrito but then again there's no such thing as too much bacon
6. Take a little bit of olive oil and pour in skillet.
7. Cut sweet potatoes into strips and throw in skillet.
8. Throw some salt/pepper and a little bit of garlic on potatoes.
9. Cook until they're heated up.
10. Scramble up 3 eggs.
11. Throw it all onto a tortilla, wrap it up and enjoy.

Serves: 1

Breakfast

Name: Amanda McGerigle

Location: raised in VT, living on Cape Cod for the last 10 years

Occupation: Gardener/landscaper

Shows Attended: 70

Favorite Song: Pre-break up: "Guyute"/2002 Since '09, "Antelope" and "Shine a Light"

Favorite Experience: I saw Phish for the first time 12/2/95. I had no idea what I was witnessing. All I remembered from that was a piano solo like none other. I realize now, it was the Squirming Coil. Didn't see Phish again till '97, the Great Went. My boyfriend at the time took me. We packed up my 86 VW Jetta and hit the road. I remember once we got onto I-95, I started seeing other cars with Phish stickers, kids with dreads and VW vans. I got so excited and felt part of something special. That weekend solidified my love of Phish. I spent my college years chasing Phish between term papers and midterms. I was hooked. I also called "Halley's Comet" to open set 3 the first day at the Went… I felt very cool :) 2009, the whole thing was a favorite Phish experience too!
Origin of recipe: A good friend made it for me one summer day. I never wanted my oatmeal cooked any other way!

Favorite memory of sharing recipe: When I make it for someone the first time, they are on board with the ingredients until I add the sour cream, then they look skeptical… until they taste it.

Song this recipe is: It would be the Zappa tune, "Peaches en Regalia," as played by Phish.

Show this recipe is: It would be 12/2/2009, because after 70 shows and 14 years to the day of my career of seeing Phish, I finally got my first Peaches en Regalia.

Strawberries en Regalia

Ingredients:
2 cups oatmeal
10 strawberries
A few tablespoons of brown sugar
Sour cream

Directions:
1. Cook 2 cups of oatmeal on your stove top.
2. Quarter 10 strawberries and place them in a bowl.
3. Add a few tablespoons of brown sugar to strawberries and stir until strawberries are coated (the berries and sugar will create a brown sugary syrup in the bottom of the bowl).
4. Divide oatmeal into 2 bowls.
5. Add strawberries.
5. Add one dollop of sour cream onto the strawberries, stir it all together and ENJOY!

This oatmeal strawberries and cream dream will keep you going through the day, until you encounter that heady veggie burrito in the lot… :)

Serves: 2

Breakfast

Name: Jeff

Location: Destin, FL

Occupation: Software Analyst

Shows Attended: 12

Favorite Song: "Sparkle"

Favorite Experience: Nothing tops my first Phish show. I had never been to a real concert, of any kind (besides Brooks & Dunn, which I don't count), and my buddies dragged me to a Phish show in 1998 (MTSU-Murfreesboro, TN). I knew I was hooked after hearing the audience/band erupt in laughter after the "My Friend" opener.

Origin of recipe: San Francisco deli, with my own spin added.

Favorite memory of sharing recipe: Me and my 5 college buddies set off on a camping trip into the Blue Ridge mountains for a spring break excursion. We ate these for breakfast each morning.

Song this recipe is: "I Am Hydrogen"

Show this recipe is: MTSU 1998. Because, if not for that show, I would not be taking the time to share my uber-awesome recipe with you all.

Poster Nutbagel

Ingredients:
½ regular bagel
1 tablespoon cream cheese
2 slices tomato
2 slices cucumber
2 basil leaves
1 teaspoon sesame seeds

Directions:
1. Spread the cream cheese onto the bagel.
2. Sprinkle on the sesame seeds.
3. Add the tomato, cucumber slices, and basil leaves.
4. Enjoy!

Serves: 1

Breakfast

you can be just as hungover, and still hospitable! In preparing them, make double of what you think you'll eat; you end up with extras, and then you cook them up for your neighbors too. This will increase your festival socialization with neighbors, which enhances festival experience!! (And they may even share with you later when you don't feel like cooking!)

Festival-Proof Breakfast Burritos

(continued)

**Suggestion: if you plan to make yours with ham, make ¼ of your burritos vegetarian… you never know who will appreciate it, and in the end an egg, salsa, and cheese burrito is still really really yummy.) Roll burrito and wrap in foil. Mark "H" with a sharpie marker for ones containing ham and "V" for vegetarian. Take the foil-wrapped burritos and put them in vacuum-seal bags, two at a time, and seal them. This prevents your food from being waterlogged no matter how many spunions grab a beer the night before. If you don't know anyone that you can borrow a vacuum sealer from, I suggest Lock-and-Lock brand containers… they won't leak ice-cold cooler water into your food, they just take up more space than a vacuum packed baggie. When you are ready to cook at the festival, turn your propane grill to medium-low, take the foil-wrapped burritos out of their plastic, and stick them on the grill. Turn over after smoking one cigarette. If you don't smoke (I am trying to quit myself), ask a friend to use this valuable sand-timer style instrument. After the cigarette is done, turn with quick fingers or a spatula. Cook the other side for half as long, flip again, and pay attention to the foil. If on low-medium heat, the foil should only start to turn brown after this long. Cook it this slowly so you can be assured that the center of the burrito is as warm as the outside.
Take the burrito off the grill but BEWARE: it will be very very hot.

Serves: 6

Entrees

Name: Randy Kramer Pierce

Location: Albany, NY

Occupation: Professional Renaissance Woman

Shows Attended: 23 and counting

Favorite Song: "Wading in the Velvet Sea"

Favorite Experience: Standing under a giant tarp with a bunch of other kids as the rain poured down during the 6/17/04 Brooklyn show… It was miraculous the way the rain just STOPPED as soon as they finished playing Maze at the end of the 1st set!!!

Origin of recipe: I started eating vegetarian when I was a freshman in high school. My family was very supportive and my mom used to make this for me for dinner all the time! It is packed with nutrients, low in fat and SOOOO delicious!

Favorite memory of sharing recipe: I flew down to Tennessee to visit my friend from college on her birthday. I cooked her this meal for her birthday dinner. She is half Indian so she LOOOOVES anything with curry in it. She said it was extra delicious because somebody else cooked for her! :)

Song this recipe is: "Gumbo"

Show this recipe is: It would be the 2nd set of the 11/28/09 Albany show @ the Knick… like the Seven Below into Ghost it is complex and dark and so so tasty!!! Oh and of course you gotta "Cool it Down" with some sour cream on top. Yum!

Curried Lentils & Sweet Potatoes

Ingredients:
1 tablespoon olive oil
1 medium yellow onion, chopped
2 garlic cloves, minced
1 tablespoon curry powder
1 teaspoon cumin
3 medium sweet potatoes (or butternut squash if you wanna change it up!), peeled & cut into 1-inch cubes
1 cup lentils, rinsed
½ cup long grain or basmati rice
½ teaspoon salt
1 can (14 ounce) vegetable or chicken broth
2 ¼ cups water
¼ cup fresh cilantro leaves
Sour cream

Directions:
1. In nonstick 12-inch skillet, heat olive oil over medium heat until hot. Add onion and cook 5 minutes, stirring often. Add garlic and curry powder, and cook 1 minute longer, stirring often.
2. Stir in sweet potatoes, lentils, rice, salt, broth, and water; heat to boiling over medium-high heat. Reduce heat to low; cover and simmer 30 minutes or until lentils and rice are tender and almost all liquid is absorbed. Let stand 5 minutes. Sprinkle with lots of cilantro and add a dollop of sour cream to serve.
3. This dish tastes great the 2nd (and 3rd… and 4th…) day, after the flavors have married… and it travels well to boot! Make an extra large batch for dinner & and then bring the leftovers to use as burrito innards if you're going to a festival for the weekend! You can reheat in a small pot or just eat it cold… put in a wrap with some tomato, sprouts, avocado and sour cream and BAM! Happy mouth. :)

Serves: 4

Entrees

Name: Suzanne Journey Blain

Location: Burlington, VT

Occupation: Art Teacher

Shows Attended: Upper 30s

Favorite Song: That's like picking a favorite child

Favorite Experience: Meatstick Reprise in Vegas 2004

Origin of recipe: I went crazy with ingredients from the bottom of the veggie drawer.

Favorite memory of sharing recipe: Eating huge bowls of it while watching the Olympics.

Song this recipe is: "Strange Design"

Show this recipe is: That Brooklyn show when Jay-Z came out, because that was sweet.

Strangely Designed Casserole

Ingredients:
4 small organic zucchinis
1 bunch of green chard
1 big onion
3 gloves of garlic
Italian mix of herbs
Olive oil
Box of spiral pasta
Big can of tomato sauce
Can of black beans
A good amount of Cabot shredded pepper jack cheese

Directions:

1. Stir fry all the green stuff.
2. Cook up the noodles.
3. In a casserole dish or two, layer the green stuff with a little bit of cheese.
4. Sprinkle a layer of beans.
5. Layer of noodles.
6. Thin layer of sauce.
7. Sprinkle the cheese on top.
8. Cover and bake at 350 degrees until the cheese melts.

Serves: 6

Entrees

Name: Jeff Mitchell

Location: Vermont

Occupation: Business Owner

Shows Attended: 100+

Favorite Song: "TMWSIY"

Favorite Experience: As far as Phish's role in my life and Hot Sauce business,Vermont Pepper Works, I found that I did/do most of my creative thinking and planning while "in that space" at shows. Phish has helped me think out of the box while keeping to my game plan and never forgetting to have phun.

Origin of recipe: While visiting the USVI on vacation, we caught some Mackerel and planned on finding a BBQ pit to fire it on. So after a generous sailor brought us on his boat and dropped us off on what seemed to be a deserted beach we ran in the "hole in the forest" and came apon some ire folks willing to let us chill and grill our fish. Needless to say, it was a great meal.

Favorite memory of sharing recipe: While sampling our sauces in the parking lots or at other venues, the expressions on people's faces, either good or bad, can be quite a good time. The range of emotion greatly varies between the people, but it is quite rewarding

when someone really gets their rocks off.

Song this recipe is: "Reba"

Show this recipe is: Big Birch Pavillion, Patterson, NY. Wednesday, July, 13, 1994. Vermont Pepper Works sauces can be deceiving by the subtle names of each sauce and bright colors, but what is inside can take one to another level of flavor, texture, and heat which has to be experienced to be understood.

St. John Fired King Fish

Ingredients:
2 to 4 servings of either Mackerel, King Fish, Mahi, or Tuna
½ cup Spanish onion small dice
1 teaspoon of fresh lime juice (¼ lime)
1 clove crushed garlic
¼ cup Vermont Pepper Works Roasted Garlic & Carrot Cayenne Pepper Sauce. Rated R

Directions:
1. Combine onion, lime, garlic and hot sauce together in a zip lock or in a container to marinate the fish.
2. Let sit for at least 30 minuets.
3. GRILL 'ER UP!!

Serves: 2-4

Entrees

Name: Anonymous

Location: Capitalism, USA

Occupation: Phan

Shows Attended: Many

Favorite Experience: The one where this recipe didn't come in to play.

Origin of recipe: I had extra tickets to a show I couldn't sell to anyone.

Favorite memory of sharing recipe: There is no positive memory associated with this dish.

Song this recipe is: "Undermind"

Show this recipe is: Detroit 11/17/09, Darien 8/14/09, Alpine Valley 7/19/03

How to Eat Tickets

Ingredients:
All the tickets you can't sell
1 tablespoon olive oil
1 can chicken broth
1 cup angostura bitters

Directions:
1. Pan sear tickets in a little olive oil.
2. Mix in chicken broth with bitters.
3. Cook in oven at 225 degrees for 3 to 5 hours.
4. Eat and try to enjoy.

Servings depend on how many tickets you got stuck with.

Entrees

Name: Jenn Kelley

Location: Farmingville, NY

Occupation: Sales Associate

Shows Attended: 20 (3 upcoming at MSG)

Favorite Song: "Silent in the Morning"

Favorite Experience: It's a tough call, but I would have to say seeing Phish on my birthday for the 20th anniversary show in Boston rocked. Happy Birthday to me.

Origin of recipe: I created it because I ordered enchiladas at a local restaurant and thought, "I can do this better." I felt that the filling needed to have more cheese and be more creamy. I added the jalapeño pepper later to give it more kick. It is a favorite among my friends and family.

Favorite memory of sharing recipe: I gave the recipe to my friend's 11 year-old-son, Brandon, who is an aspiring chef. Since my friend does not cook, he always enjoys trying new recipes. He and I often talk recipes and share our favorite Food Network episodes with one another.

Song this recipe is: "Mexican Cousin"

Jennchiladas

Ingredients:
1 pound boneless chicken breasts, cooked and shredded
2 packages cream cheese
2 cups cheddar cheese, shredded
2 cups Monterey jack cheese, shredded
1 can chopped chilis
1 jalapeño, minced
3 cloves garlic, minced
⅓ cup water
3 tablespoons olive oil
Enchilada sauce (2 to 3 small cans Ortega)
2 cups heavy cream or half and half
6 tortilla wraps
Yellow saffron rice (optional)
Black beans (optional)
Sour cream on the side
Guacamole on the side
Shredded lettuce

Directions:
1. Boil chicken breasts for approximately 20 minutes. Let cool slightly to allow for easier shredding. Shred and set aside.
2. Put olive oil in large skillet.
3. Add minced garlic, chilis and jalapeño (I put all 3 in food processor to make it really fine)
4. Sauté in oil until slightly softened.
5. Add cream cheese until melted.
6. Add 1 cup cheddar cheese and 1 cup Monterey jack cheese, and when just about fully melted, add water.
7. Mix well until all melted and then add shredded chicken and heat.
8. Put chicken mixture, a scoop of rice and a scoop of beans and additional cheese if desired, into tortilla wrap.
9. Fold over and place face down in a 9x13 in. pan.
10. Pour half and half and enchilada sauce over the top of each jennchilada.
11. Sprinkle remaining cheese over the top.
12. Bake uncovered for 30 to 35 minutes at 350 degrees.
13. Top with shredded lettuce and serve with sour cream & guacamole.

Serves: 6

Entrees

Name: Tyler Comeaux

Location: Houston, TX

Occupation: Logistics

Shows Attended: 21

Favorite Song: If I must pick one it would be "Harry Hood"

Favorite Experience: I would have to say my first show, which was the New Orleans Jazz and Heritage festival in April of 1996. It was just a wonderful experience and boy did it get me hooked on Phish. Every other experience since then has been incredible but I will always look back on that one as one of the best times of my life.

Origin of recipe: Family recipe that I learned from my Dad but have tweaked a bit.

Favorite memory of sharing recipe: One Friday after Thanksgiving we made a version of this, substituting the chicken with leftover turkey. My brother and I woke up at 8 and even made our own turkey stock. It was a beautiful crisp Fall day here in Houston and was just a great time working in the kitchen and enjoying several cold ones with my bro throughout the process. By the time the gumbo was complete we were hammered and the gumbo was a great success; everyone loved it.

Song this recipe is: "Gumbo"

Show this recipe is: Let's go with the 4/26/96 show in New Orleans. It's fitting since this is a regional dish for Louisiana.

Ain't No Time To Stash The Chicken And Sausage Gumbo

Ingredients:
2 to 3 tablespoons vegetable oil
1 package of your favorite smoked beef sausage, sliced into bite sized pieces
½ cup all-purpose flour
Salt and pepper
Cayenne pepper
Tony Chachere's Creole seasoning
1 package boneless skinless chicken thighs (about 12 thighs), cut into bite-size pieces
2 medium white onions, chopped
2 green bell peppers, chopped
2 ribs of celery, chopped
5 to 6 cloves garlic, chopped
2 bay leaves
10 to 12 cups chicken stock
Hot sauce (recommend Tabasco)
Scallions, sliced
2 cups rice, cooked

Directions:
Heat a large cast-iron pot (dutch oven) over medium heat and add the vegetable oil. Once oil is heated well, start cooking the sausage until browned. Using a slotted spoon, remove the sausage to a plate or bowl. Season the pieces of chicken thighs liberally with Tony Chachere's, salt and pepper. Begin browning the chicken in the pot, making sure not to overcrowd the pot. You want to ensure that the chicken browns, and this will not happen if the pot is crowded; cook in batches if necessary. Once chicken is browned, remove from the pot into a bowl. Add the flour to the pot to make a roux and stir continously with a wooden spoon for approx. thirty minutes or about the amount of time it takes to drink two beers. You want your roux to achieve the color of milk chocolate. Once roux looks like milk chocolate, add the onions, celery and bell peppers ("the trinity" as it's called in Louisiana). Season vegetables with a tablespoon of salt and some fresh cracked pepper. Once the vegetables soften a bit (about 10 minutes), add the garlic. Cook the garlic for about 3 minutes making sure you do not burn it. Add the chicken stock and bring up to a boil. If mixture is too thick for your liking, feel free to add more chicken stock to thin it out. Once it comes up to a boil, reduce heat and add another dash of salt and pepper and about a teaspoon of cayenne. Reduce the heat to a simmer and cook uncovered for an hour. Return chicken and sausage to the pot. Cook uncovered for another hour until chicken is cooked through. Taste for seasoning and adjust if needed. If you like more heat you can add a couple of dashes of hot sauce at this point. Drop heat to low and place lid on pot. At this point cook the two cups of rice in four cups of either water or chicken stock. Spoon rice into bowl and ladle gumbo on top of it. Garnish with sliced scallion. I recommend serving with warm French bread.

Serves: 10

Entrees

Name: Drew Suto

Location: Troy, NY

Occupation: Stay-at-home Dad.

Shows Attended: 154

Favorite Song: "Buffalo Bill"

Favorite Experience: Worcester '98 Run

Origin of recipe: I came up with it a few years ago. I have made it from time to time.

Favorite memory of sharing recipe: My wife being like, "What are you putting in it?" and then her liking it very much.

Song this recipe is: "Meat"

Show this recipe is: The BOMB factory.

The Gordon Burger

Ingredients:
1 pound lean ground beef
2 half sour kosher dill pickles, chopped fine
2 tablespoons minced garlic
1 large egg
¼ cup breadcrumbs
5 pieces of crispy bacon chopped fine
2 pieces of gouda cheese, sliced 1 inch thick, or any kind of cheese you want
Mayonnaise
Large kaiser rolls

Directions:
Preheat oven to 300 degrees. In a large mixing bowl, beat egg 'til mixed well. Add pickles, garlic and bacon. Mix well. Add ground beef and knead well over and over again. Add breadcrumbs and knead some more 'til all seems to be spread through. Make two large patties. You can cook these on a grill or in a pan, whichever you choose to do. When the burgers are cooked how you like, then take them and place into a pan. Put cheese on top and place in oven for a few minutes. Keep an eye on them while the cheese melts. Meanwhile, you can spread a little mayonnaise on the inside of your rolls or whatever you prefer; mayo always seems good but some people don't like it. Take burgers out of oven and place on rolls. Serve with blue corn chips and a sweet salsa of your liking. Eat and enjoy the Gordon Burger.

Serves: 2

Entrees

Name: Possum Pete

Location: Pennsylvania

Occupation: Street Sweeper

Shows Attended: 32

Favorite Song: "Possum"

Origin of recipe: Family recipe, our road always had dead possums and we were poor.

Favorite memory of sharing recipe: People eating and raving about this until I tell them it is made from possum roadkill.

Song this recipe is: "Possum"

As seen in PhanArt: The Art of the Fans of Phish

Pennsylvania Possum Pot Pie

Ingredients:
Five-pound possum, cut into serving pieces
Water
Salt
12 peppercorns
2 ribs celery, chopped
2 carrots, quartered
1 onion
2 cups flour
4 egg yolks
6 tablespoons hot water

Directions:
Place possum in kettle. Add water to cover, salt to taste, peppercorns, celery, carrots and onion. Simmer until possum is thoroughly tender, about two hours. Strain broth and pour into clean kettle. Simmer while preparing remaining ingredients. Remove possum from bones. Discard bones and skin. Cut possum into bite-size pieces. Sift flour and one-half teaspoon salt together onto board. Make well in center and put egg yolks into it. Gradually work yolks into flour until stiff dough is formed, adding hot water as needed. Knead until smooth, about five minutes. Cut dough in half. Roll each half until paper thin. Cut dough into noodles about one inch wide. Add possum to simmering broth. Gradually add noodles. Continue boiling until noodles are done, about five minutes.

Serves: 12

Entrees

Name: Josh Faulds

Location: Boone, NC

Occupation: Sales Manager for Alternative Energy Company

Shows Attended: 20…got into 'em kinda late :-(. But doing more every tour!

Favorite Song: "Reba" or "David Bowie"

Favorite Experience: Not one particular experience, but a magical moment that happens at shows. The moment at a show when the energy flowing back and forth between the band and the audience becomes so big and overwhelming that it blurs the lines of who it's flowing from, and there is just an amazing feeling of energy going through everybody there….and you can see it in the smiles all around you and the smiles on the band members. Nothing beats it!

Origin of recipe: The recipe comes from a friend's girlfriend. My friend and his girlfriend are both natives of St. Thomas, Virgin Islands, and the recipe is from her family.
THIS IS PERFECT LOT FOOD!

Favorite memory of sharing recipe: My favorite memory is making it for some West Indian friends (people from Trinidad, Jamaica, Dominica and the Virgin Islands), and having them give me the thumbs up. It let me know it was as good as the natives do it and it made me feel great.

Song this recipe is: "Ghost" (warm, chunky and thick…like some good cow funk)

Show this recipe is: It would be 11/17/97, Denver, CO. The food, much like the show, is experimental but is incredibily smooth and filled with warm chunky goodness all the way through and with a great finish (i.e. YEM).

Colonel Forbin's Caribbean Chicken Roti

Ingredients:
3 boneless chicken breats, cut into chunks
2 ½ potatoes, cut into cubes
1 large carrot, sliced thinly
1 large red onion, chopped chunky
½ green pepper, chopped chunky
½ yellow pepper, chopped chunky
1 can diced green chilis (for flavor, add to taste)
16 ounces chicken broth
6 cloves of crushed garlic
2 ½ tablespoons Jamaican yellow curry powder
Salt & fresh-ground pepper (to taste)
4 large flour tortillas
1 jar mango chutney

Directions:
1. In a large skillet, sauté garlic and onion for 1 to 2 minutes. Add chicken chunks and sauté a few minutes until cooked but still very tender. Add green pepper, yellow pepper, carrots, and green chilis and let sauté 2 minutes. Add potatoes, chicken broth, and as much water is needed to barely cover everything. Simmer until the potatoes are very tender, and begin to reduce broth. Stir in curry powder and any other spices you may want while potatoes are simmering (salt, pepper, onion powder). Let simmer.
2. Cover and turn off. This should now stand for a while so that it can thicken up as it cools down. You want it to be a thick stew. Reduce more if too runny.
3. When ready to eat, heat back up the roti mixture on stove. Warm your tortillas, place on plate and spoon roti mixture into center of tortillas. Fold into a "burrito-like" shape and top with healthy portion of mango chutney.

Serves: 4

Entrees

Name: Jennifer St. Germain

Location: Connecticut

Occupation: Deaf Education

Shows Attended: Too many to count

Favorite Song: "NICU"

Favorite Experience: Seeing the boys play a stealth show under the name The Third Ball at Joyous Lake in Woodstock, NY on June 6, 1996. :)

Origin of recipe: I probably saw or ate it somewhere, but let's just leave it at "I'm a culinary genius."

Favorite memory of sharing recipe: My crew always brings a ton of food that we all share with each other. Every show is like a hippie potluck! I get a real sense of satisfaction when my friends really love eating something I made and want the recipe. <3

Song this recipe is: "You Enjoy Myself"

Show this recipe is: IT. Because my dish is the sh-IT

You Enjoy My Spicy Thai Peanut Noodles

Ingredients:
Wide egg noodles
Cucumbers, halved, seeded and sliced
Shredded carrots
Bean sprouts
(shredded chicken breast is optional)
Spicy Thai peanut sauce:
1 cup smooth, organic peanut butter
½ cup warm water
1 tablespoon fish oil
2 to 3 tablespoons soy sauce
2 cloves of garlic, mashed and minced
Sriracha HOT chili sauce (however spicy you like it. I like it HOT) a.k.a., cock sauce :)
1 teaspoon fresh lemon juice

Directions:
1. Make the peanut sauce and set aside.
2. Boil the noodles and prepare the veggies (you can add more veggies if you like).
*I don't mix all the ingredients until I'm just about to serve. I put the noodles in a gallon Ziploc bag and prepare my veggies at the show.
*I prepare the peanut sauce at home and put it in a non-glass container. An empty peanut butter jar works perfectly!!
4. Mix together noodles, veggies and peanut sauce and enjoy.
**if the peanut sauce thickens up on you, just add a little more warm water. :)

Serves: 8

Entrees

Name: Robin Thompson

Location: F.L.O.R.I.D.A.

Occupation: Financial Counselor

Shows Attended: 1

Favorite Song: Can't help it, "Waste."

Origin of recipe: The Magic Bullet infomercial gave me the idea for a healthy meal that didn't involve cooking.

Swamp Noodles

Ingredients:
1 box of whole wheat pasta
3 cups fresh basil
2 cloves of garlic
⅓ cup of pine nuts
¼ cup of grated parmesan cheese
½ cup extra virgin olive oil

Directions:
1. Cook pasta.
2. Blend remaining ingredients together in a food processor.
3. Add salt and pepper to taste.
4. Pour over whole wheat pasta.

Serves: 4

Entrees

Name: Julie Parker

Location: Originally Germany, then Florida then Texas then Indiana

Occupation: Web content analyst

Shows Attended: 95 (As of Summer 2010)

Favorite Song: "First Tube"

Favorite Experience: New Year's Eve '03, Miami, 9th row. I snuck a 9 foot inflatable cactus into the AAA and my best friend and I (and several people in our row) blew it up in the hopes that we could get it passed up to the stage and stood next to Mike (yeah, yeah, if you're gonna dream, might as well dream big, right?). Unfortunately it didn't make it, but we had so much fun trying!

Origin of recipe: My family is Italian, but I lived in Texas for 8 years and I love, love, love Mexican food! So, this is a Mexican spin on an Italian favorite. Warning! This recipe makes A LOT (I have a big family!), so if it's just 4 people or less, I'd suggest cutting it in half.

Favorite memory of sharing recipe: The first time I made it was when I was visiting my aunt, uncle and 2 cousins in Florida and they LOVED it! This is a die-hard Italian food eatin' family, so of course I was

thrilled they liked my variation! :)

Song this recipe is: "Mexican Cousin"

Show this recipe is: 6/17/04, Brooklyn, Keyspan Park. It POURED the ENTIRE show….buckets and buckets of rain…but we had so much fun we didn't even care. I think you'll like the Mexican spin on this so much, you won't even notice it's not Italian! :)

Mexican Cousin Manicotti

Ingredients:
2 8 ounce packages shredded Monterey jack (or your favorite Mexican blend) cheese
2 cans vegetarian refried beans
20 uncooked manicotti noodles
2 cups water
2 jars of enchilada sauce
16 ounces tomato sauce
1 cup sour cream
1 large tomato
½ cup green onion, sliced
½ cup sliced pitted olives
**For non-vegetarian variety
1 pound lean ground beef
1 package dry taco seasoning

Directions:
1. In a bowl, combine 3 cups of cheese and both cans of refried beans.
2. Stuff uncooked pasta tubes with cheese/bean mixture, pressing firmly into shells. A trick to load the shells easily is to put your bean/cheese mixture into a large Ziploc bag and then cut one of the corners so it acts like a pastry bag. This is less messy too!
3. In a microwave-safe dish, combine water, enchilada sauce and tomato sauce.
4. Microwave on HIGH until mixture is steaming hot (about 5 to 6 minutes).
5. You'll need two 9x13 in. pans for this recipe. Using half the sauce, pour equal amounts of the sauce into each pan.
6. Place 10 uncooked stuffed tubes in each pan, turning each to coat with sauce.
7. Using the other half of the sauce, pour equal amounts of the sauce over the stuffed noodles in each pan.
8. Cover and bake at 375 degrees for 20 minutes.
9. Turn shells over.
10. Continue baking, covered, for 20 minutes.
11. Uncover, top each pan with equal parts of the remaining cheese.
12. Bake 4 to 5 minutes longer or until cheese is completely melted.
**For non-vegetarian variety, cook ground beef and taco seasoning together and spread evenly in equal amounts over each 9x13 in. pan.
13. Dollop with sour cream and sprinkle with onions, olives and diced tomatoes.

Serves: 8

Entrees

Name: Terry Mason

Location: Loudonville, NY

Occupation: Homemaker

Shows Attended: 0

Favorite Song: "Halley's Comet"

Origin of recipe: Came from a good friend!!

Four Pepper Pasta

Ingredients:
1 box penne pasta, cooked
1 large red pepper
1 large yellow pepper
1 large green pepper
1 large sweet onion
3 tablespoons olive oil
1 tablespoon sugar
3 tablespoons balsamic vinegar or red wine vinegar
¾ teaspoon dried basil leaves, or several fresh basil leaves
½ teaspoon black pepper

Directions:

1. Cut peppers and onions into ½ inch strips.
2. In 12 inch skillet, cook peppers and onions in olive oil until tender.
3. Add salt and cook until veggies begin to brown.
4. Stir in sugar, vinegar, basil and pepper. Heat through.
5. Toss with pasta and enjoy!

Serves: 6

Entrees

Name: Pete Mason

Location: Albany, NY

Occupation: Teacher

Shows Attended: 77 as of August 2010

Favorite Song: "Harry Hood" and "The Meatstick"

Favorite Experience: Summer tour 2003, driving from Atlanta to Pittsburgh and then Albany with my brother Chris before heading to IT.

Origin of recipe: I have always loved chili. I started in high school, then in '03 I made it a yearly event each fall, make a huge pot of chili, invite everyone over for football and tasty chili with great beer, and the recipe has found perfection.

Favorite memory of sharing recipe: Having people coming over to enjoy the chili and hang out for the day

Song this recipe is: "MEAT!"

Show this recipe is: Big Cypress, because this chili has a little bit of EVERYTHING in it, and it's so damn good when you are done with it. Also, like Big Cypress, any other attempt to make chili as good pales in comparison.

Mason's Chili(dren)

Ingredients:
This makes a good 20+ servings, enough for many hungry folks and leftovers to last through winter. You can split the recipe in half, but it is best to make a large pot for all to enjoy!

2 green peppers
1 red onion
4 white onions
2 cans stewed tomatoes
1 large can crushed tomatoes
1 can tomato paste
1 jar jalapeños
1 jar banana peppers
1 can kidney beans (light)
1 can kidney beans (dark)
2 cans black beans (black)
2 chicken breasts
1 pound sweet sausage
1 pound beef stew chunks
1 pound ground beef
½ pound bacon
2 tablespoons sugar
1 tablespoon oregano
1 teaspoon cumin
3 teaspoons pepper
2 teaspoons salt
1 tablespoon chili powder
¼ cup cayenne pepper
2 tablespoons cilantro
1 teaspoon basil
1 teaspoon thyme
3 tablespoons garlic powder
2 tablespoons paprika
3 tablespoons cocoa powder
½ cup yellow mustard
Misc: one can light beer (Bud Light recommended), 1 bottle Dinosaur BBQ slathering sauce,
2 shots Tequila (whatever you prefer),
1 12 ounce bottle of Frank's Red Hot Sauce, (no substitutions on this one!),
1 12 ounce bottle A1, 12 ounce bottle of lime juice, Olive Oil, Rice - 6 bags of Boil-in-bag rice works for this size recipe, sour cream, grated cheese, sharp cheddar works best.

(*Recipe continued on page 133*)

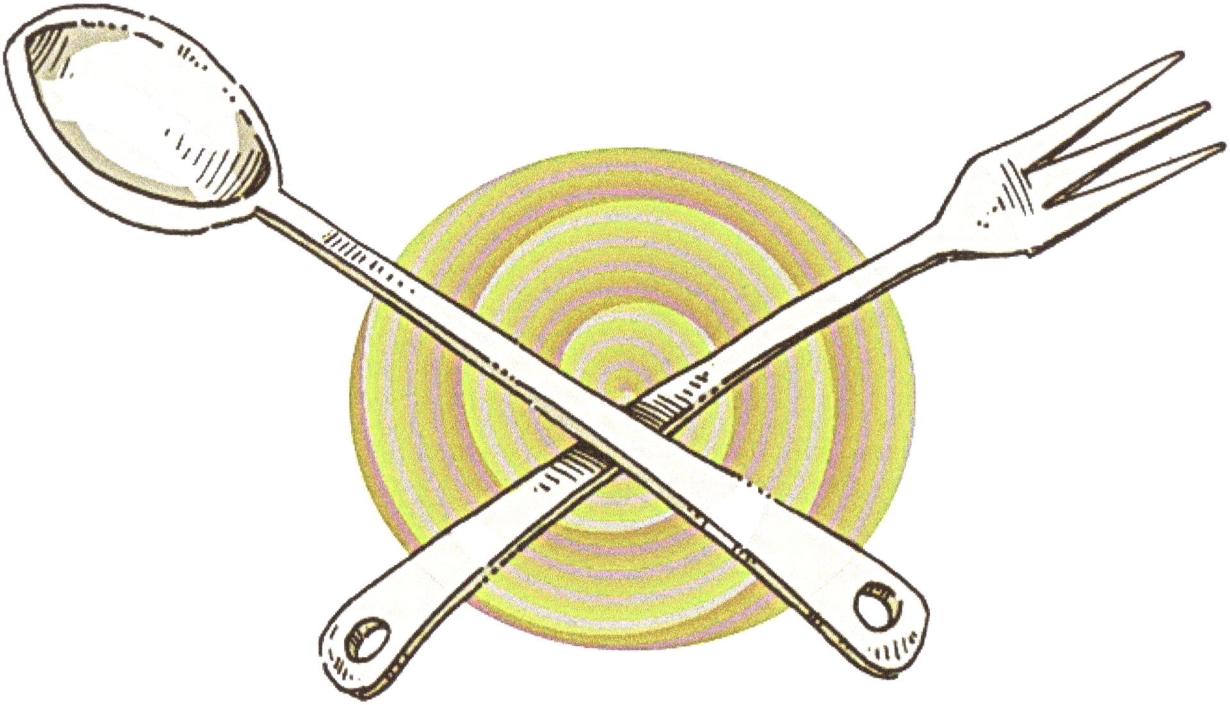

Illustration: *Cody Schibi*

Mason's Chili(dren)

(continued)

Directions:

You need a GIANT chili pot for this. I use a 5 gallon pot and have had room to spare.

Meat: Chicken: Boil chicken breasts in tequila, juice from the jar of banana peppers and lime juice, with a dash of pepper. While chicken boils, chop up in pot, allowing for chunks and shreds of chicken. Boil until all juice is gone, put in giant pot (this means the aforementioned giant chili pot, but if you want, go ahead and add in those other herbs. Not recommended though)

Beef chunks: Cut beef stew chunks up into smaller pieces. Cook beef stew chunks in A1 sauce until well done. The meat HAS to be well done for this part.

Ground Beef: Cook 1 pound ground beef. When done, drain fat, pour in ½ the bottle of Dino BBQ sauce and reserve the rest for later. Cook on low heat for 10 more minutes.

Sweet sausage: Coat sweet sausage in olive oil, place in pan with foil cover, cook in oven at 400 degrees for 30 minutes, checking on it, chopping it, and chunking it while it cooks.

Bacon: Cook ½ pound until crispy and even slightly burned, a little burn here is very OK.

Take all the meat, put it in the pot, and then…

Veggies: Chop 2 green peppers julienne style (strips). Purée 2 white onions till soupy. Chop 2 white onions loosely. Chop red onion chunky. Add all these to the pot.

Add to this: Kidney beans, black beans, stewed tomatoes, crushed tomatoes, tomato paste, yellow mustard, jar of jalapeños (some juice is ok), banana peppers (ditto), beer, hot sauce, rest of A1, rest of Dino BBQ sauce, any leftover lime juice.

Spices: add all spices, plus cocoa powder to the pot.

Bring the entire pot to a boil.

Stir with a wooden spoon and cover once well blended. Keep stirring, on low heat, for 2 hours.

Adjust according to taste using crusty Italian bread.

Top with grated cheese and sour cream, crack a tasty beer and enjoy!

Serves: 20 (prep time - 1 hour, cook time - 2 hours)

Entrees

Name: Eric Stombaugh

Location: Stevens, Pennsylvania

Occupation: Owner/partner

Shows Attended: 299

Favorite Song: Don't have one.

Favorite Experience: Virginia Beach encore 8/9/98 & Fuji rock festival

Origin of recipe: A very simple family recipe I learned at a very young age from my great grandmother. Side note: before seeing Phish at the Ukrainian National Home in NYC in '89, I was eating there & an older woman came out of the kitchen - I was with an older cousin & she commented to the woman how good the haluski was, especially the noodles. I started talking to the woman about differences between Ukrainian & Croatian food (I'm Croatian in descent) & upon comparing recipes, her noodles are the same as my great grandmother's.

Favorite memory of sharing recipe: Obviously my childhood memories with family but most recently, it has proven to be a loved dish among my vegetarian friends.

Song this recipe is: "YEM"

Show this recipe is: 7/16/98-Prague
It would've been the closest Phish ever got to where this recipe came from & I love this show!

GG's Haluski

Ingredients:
1 med head of cabbage, cored & chopped
1 med/lg spanish/yellow onion, chopped into large dice
1 stick butter quartered
Salt
Pepper
NOODLES:
2 lg eggs
2 ½ cup flour sifted
½ cup milk
½ cup water
Pinch salt
Pinch baking powder

Directions:

1. Combine dry ingredients. Combine wet ingredients. Slowly add wet to dry until sticky dough is formed. Using spoons, drop small portions of dough (size is up to your personal taste - I usually stay around the size of a standard gnocchi) into well-salted boiling water. Noodles are done after they float for a couple seconds. Remove noodles as they are finished to a paper-towel-lined bowl.
2. In a large dutch oven or heavy skillet, put a good sweat on a nice size yellow onion with a ½ stick of butter, salt & pepper. Add chopped head of cabbage & sauté until lightly browning/tender. Add noodles, ½ stick of butter & cook on med/low for at least 30 minutes. Stir periodically & season with salt & pepper.

Serves: 6

Entrees

Name: Joel Cummins & Dasha Davis

Location: Chicago, currently

Occupation: Musician & Event Specialist

Shows Attended: hmm… 5 together and about 20-30 each before then

Favorite Song: "Reba"

Favorite Experience: MSG NYE 1995. Amazing show.

Recipe Name: Vegan Creamed Spinach

Origin of recipe: Vegan recipe we found online!

Favorite memory of sharing recipe: We've made them once for each other. Making dinner at home together can be a lot of fun for two people who travel all the time.

Song this recipe is: "Weigh"

Show this recipe is: Come on now.

Vegan Creamed Spinach Surprise

Ingredients:
½ container (6 to 8) button mushrooms, diced
½ finely chopped small white onion
1 clove minced garlic
Vegan butter/margarine
1 ¼ cup water
Fresh grated nutmeg
1 pint plain soy milk
2 pkg frozen chopped spinach, drained and thawed
1 teaspoon corn starch
1 spaghetti squash, approximate size of a football
Olive oil
Sea salt
Pepper
1 oval or square casserole dish 8 to 9"
Halved cherry tomatoes

(*Recipe continued on page 139*)

Drinks

Name: Brad Ecke

Location: New Jersey

Occupation: Student

Shows Attended: 9

Favorite Song: "Weekapaug Groove"

Favorite Experience: NYE 2009

Origin of recipe: I'm a bartender, boring night at work.

Favorite memory of sharing recipe: Pregame party, Phish at Jones Beach, 6/2/09

Song this recipe is: It's "Ice"

Show this recipe is: Big Cypress, because it keeps the party going all night.

Phish Bowl

Ingredients:
1 gallon goldfish bowl
1 cup Nerds candy
10 shots vodka
10 shots coconut rum
1 cup blue Curaçao
1 ½ cups sweet and sour mix
4 cups pineapple juice
4 cups Sprite
1 lemon
1 lime
1 orange
1 pack Swedish fish

Directions:
1. Put the Nerds in first so it gives the same effect as gravel.
2. Combine all liquid ingredients and ice.
3. Finish with Swedish fish and lemon, lime, and orange slices.

Serves: 10

Drinks

Name: Lindsey Lustig

Location: Concord, CA

Occupation: Nutrition consultant, health educator, yoga instructor

Shows Attended: 12

Favorite Song: "AC/DC Bag"

Favorite Experience: Dancing with friends!

Origin of recipe: I made it up along with others for a project in the works.

Favorite memory of sharing recipe: Having good friends over to chill and surprising them with a healthy, tasty drink.

Song this recipe is: "Sour Grapes McGee"

Show this recipe is: A rainy, yet invigorating one because it's refreshing and cleansing.

The Sour Grape

Ingredients:
Dash of apple cider vinegar
¼ glass of organic grape juice (no sugar added)
Rest of glass with filtered water

Directions:
1. Mix and enjoy!

Serves: 1

Drinks

Name: Adam Lebin & Malaika Marion

Location: Chicago, IL. *The Brown Sack, Soup, Sandwich & Shake Shack*

Occupation: Restaurant owners

Shows Attended: 90 plus

Favorite Song: "Col. Forbin's Ascent"

Favorite Experience: Alpine 1997. This show is hosed from beginning to end.

Origin of recipe: Served at our restaurant *The Brown Sack Soup, Sandwich & Shake Shack* in the Logan Square neighborhood of Chicago

Favorite memory of sharing recipe: Seeing the smile after someone tastes the smoothie reminds me of the glow everyone has after a killer show.

Song this recipe is: It's "Ice" because of the use of ice as a main ingredient.

Show this recipe is: 11/4/1996, Hilton Coliseum Ames, Iowa. Huge ice storm took place this night with many accidents and late arrivals, for which the boys rewarded the crowd with a short but sweet show with a rare Stash encore.

It's Ice Oatmeal Smoothie

Ingredients:
7 teaspoons quick oats
¾ banana, sliced thin
2 tablespoons honey
Vanilla soy milk
Ice

Directions:

1. Use a 16 ounce cup to measure in.
2. Fill cup ¾ with ice.
3. Add 6 teaspoons of quick oats.
4. Slice ¾ of a banana on top.
5. Fill with vanilla soy milk until liquid reaches ¾ mark of cup.
6. Add 2 tablespoons of honey on top.
7. Blend until ice is broken up.
8. Pour and enjoy.

Serves: 1

Drinks

Name: Daniela "Coconut Boogaloo" Wotke

Location: Berkeley, CA

Occupation: Nurse Practitioner

Shows Attended: 24

Favorite Song: "Brother"

Favorite Experience: Finally "getting it" at Hampton '98

Origin of recipe: Crafted as a part of a group brewing day for Phantasy Tour in 2005.

Favorite memory of sharing recipe: Giving bottles of the finished product to PTers at shows.

Song this recipe is: "All Things Considered"

Show this recipe is: Uh, too obscure. I give up.

SIIHB Stout

Ingredients:
"SIIHB Stout" - extract/partial mash
6 pounds amber liquid malt extract
1 pound dark dry malt extract
12 ounce chocolate malt
4 ounce black patent
8 ounce crystal 90L
8 ounces to 16 ounces flaked oats (optional: toasted in oven for 1 hour at 300 degrees)
1 ½ ounce fuggles hops bittering
1 ½ ounce fuggles hops flavoring (Or any available hops, adjust to approx. 40 IBUs)
Yeast of your choice–American or California ale yeast for fruity/hoppy flavor, British yeast for maltier flavor.
Optional fun stuff:
1 teaspoon. Irish moss (clarifies the beer)
8-16 ounce lactose (makes it milky/creamy/sweet)
8-16 ounce cold-infused coffee (steep 2 tablespoons coffee per eight ounces cold water overnight)
Cherries, orange peels, rosemary, anything you desire

Directions:
Steep your grains and oats in a grain bag in 1 ½ to 2 gallons of water at 150 degrees for 45 minutes. At the same time, start heating up your big brew pot (with about 2 more gallons of water in it). After the grains are done steeping, dump that water into the big pot, and sparge the grains (pour a little more 150 degree water over them to rinse them into the big pot). Then, fire it up until it boils! Then turn off the heat, add the extract and bittering hops, stir a lot, then crank the heat back up. Bring to a rolling boil for 60 minutes. Then add the flavoring hops (as well as the Irish moss and lactose if you are using them) and boil for another 15 minutes. remove from heat and place into an ice bath (or run through a wort chiller). Funnel into your primary carboy and add water to make 5 gallons. Pitch your yeast when the batch is under 75 degrees. Ferment for about a week, then transfer to secondary container (if you have it) until final gravity is reached (or about 3 weeks). Your transition to secondary container is a good time to add stuff like the coffee and spices. You can also add these things at the end of your boil instead if you are concerned about contamination. Bottle or keg as usual. Finally, don't forget to SIIHB and send us some #1s.

Serves: 20

Drinks

Name: Pete Mason

Location: Albany, NY

Occupation: Teacher, all around good guy

Shows Attended: 77 as of August 2010

Favorite Song: "Meatstick!"

Favorite Experience: For this one, I'll go with 12/31/03, 4th row for NYE, best prank ever!

Origin of recipe: 12/30/09, I was digging mojitos, but wanted to mix it up a bit. Added a few other ingredients and BAM, the PhanArtini was born.

Favorite memory of sharing recipe: Sharing it on 12/30/09 and 12/31/09

Song this recipe is: "Loving Cup" (I know, a cover, but it's the only drinking song I could think of.)

Show this recipe is: 12/30/09, where it was born.

PhanArtini

Ingredients:
2 fresh mint leaves
1 teaspoon of sugar
Splash of water
1 shot vodka
Splash of tequila
Lots of ice
Splash of pineapple juice
½ can Red Bull
Soda water

Directions:
1. Muddle the mint with sugar and a splash of water.
2. Add in a shot of vodka and a half shot of tequila.
3. Fill with TONS OF ICE, ½ can Red Bull and top off with soda water.
4. Add a splash of pineapple juice and stir (don't shake).
5. ENJOY!

Serves: 1

Drinks

Name: Charlie Dirksen

Location: San Francisco

Occupation: Lawyer

Shows Attended: 85?

Favorite Song: Countless "Favorites"

Favorite Experience: In early July 1993 I saw the movie "Being There" (with Peter Sellers) and, at a pivotal point in the film, Strauss's ALSO SPRACH ZARATHUSTRA (a.k.a. 2001) is played. I told my friend Dave that I'd love to hear a band jam 2001 out *LIVE* sometime. Me and Dave were at the Wolf Trap gig, 12th row or so, only weeks after seeing "Being There." We went NUTS when Phish started up 2001- Phish had only just debuted it and I had no idea they were covering it. A life-changing experience! After that show, for years, I tried to collect every Phish show I could get on tape, and tried to see every Phish show that I could.

Origin of recipe: The traditional White Russian began to bore me, so I started to experiment.

Song this recipe is: "BDTNL"

Show this recipe is: 12/31/95, MSG. I had trouble seeing after that show, and after a few DOG LOGs, you'll have trouble seeing as well.

Dog Log

Ingredients:
2 ounces vodka
2 ounces half-and-half
1 ounce Kahlua
½ ounce Bailey's
1 teaspoon chocolate syrup
2 tablespoons of cherry juice (optional)
1 scoop Phish Food ice cream (optional)

Directions:
1. Combine all ingredients in a shaker with a handful of ice cubes.
2. Shake like hell for at least 15 seconds.
3. Pour entire contents of shaker into a tall glass or share it with another person in rocks glasses, and add more ice if you'd like.
4. Consume.

*An alternative method of serving this drink is to strain the contents of the shaker into a few martini glasses and add a few cherries. During the yuletide holiday, egg-nog may replace the half and half. TREAT THIS BEVERAGE WITH RESPECT, OR IT WILL DISRESPECT YOU. Have one too many of these, and you won't be able to read the words on this page. If you find this drink too strong, subtract some vodka and add half-and-half. Also, as with most recipes, the finer the ingredients, the more delicious the result, so don't hesitate to use Grey Goose vodka and organic half and half to make your Dog Log the BEST VERSION EVER!

Serves: 2

Drinks

Name: Amy F. Fischer

Location: Albany, NY

Occupation: you name it

Shows Attended: 89 as of end of Fall 2009 tour

Favorite Song: "Divided Sky"

Favorite Experience: 12/31/03- NYE in Miami - I was still psyched from seeing George Clinton and P Funk for the first time the night before and couldn't imagine what Phish could possibly do to top it for me. Earlier that day at my hotel I was able to enjoy a marching band practicing on a roof of another building. Back in high school in New Hartford, NY, I was a snare and quad drummer in a competitive field marching band, so it was nice to hear them practice. I had questioned what kind of event would have a marching band perform on New Year's Eve…So when Phish broke out with a Jungle Boogie, and the Mini-Cooper was lowered onto the stage, and the Miami Palmetto Senior High Band emerged from the car one by one like from a clown car, blasting out Jungle Boogie from their horns and their drums, I honestly felt that somehow Phish played the show for me. Just for me. Feel the Heat!

Origin of recipe: I was introduced to the recipe at my friend Abbi's wedding in Vermont this past summer. It

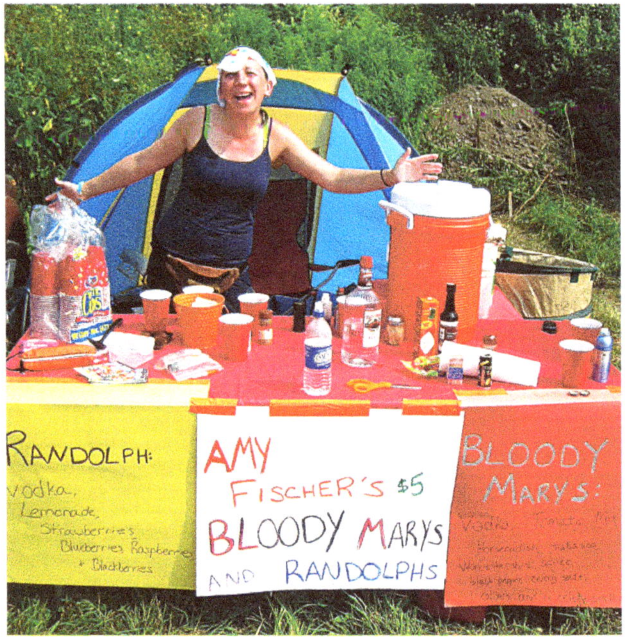

was "invented" by the groom, Mike Winters, his best pal Bill Buyer, and Abbi. Apparently they wanted to make drinks one day but had no ice. They were bright enough to use frozen berries as ice cubes. I assume they were in Randolph, VT at the time, which explains the name.

Favorite memory of sharing recipe: I have been known to sell Bloody Marys at festivals, but sometimes it's just too hot and too late in the afternoon to enjoy a spicy thick tomato drink. That's when the Randolph shines. It is the perfect drink for a blazing hot afternoon at a festival.

Song this recipe is: "Loving Cup"

The Randolph

Ingredients:
29 ounces powdered Country Time lemonade mix
Lots of vodka (unless you like virgin Randolphs, which are still refreshing)
multiple 16 ounces bags of frozen berries.
*I recommend the medley of strawberries, blueberries, blackberries, and raspberries.

Directions:
Pour two shots of vodka into a 16 ounces cup. Add lemonade and a generous scoop of frozen berries. As the berries defrost, your drink gets tastier! And then you get to enjoy the berries at the end. Very healthy festival eating!
Vending to the masses:
Fill a 5-gallon drink jug ¾ full with ice (the kind of jug with a spout that holds the drinking water at your little league games).
Dump in the entire 29 ounces bottle of lemonade mix.
Fill the jug with water and stir.
Keep the vodka separate so you can monitor how much you want in each drink.
Fill each 16 ounce cup with two shots of vodka, the ice cold lemonade, and a healthy scoop of frozen berries.
When the berries defrost after a few days in your cooler, you may want to add ice to your cup, but the bright side is the drink is fantastic from the first sip 'til the last.

Serves: 1

Drinks

Name: Brent Quickel

Location: Wilmington, NC

Shows Attended: 82

Favorite Song: "Tweezer," except on Sundays, then "Slave."

Favorite Experience: It is a toss up between the 12/4/99 Split Open And Melt and the SPAC 2004 Twist.

Origin of recipe: A good friend Matt's birthday happened to fall on the day of the return at Hampton (3/6/09). As a present to him, I brewed his favorite style of beer and let him name the beer. We convened in Hampton and the rest is history. The beer was designed as an American IPA with subtle features of English malt profiles.

Favorite memory of sharing recipe: Hampton 2009 was a very joyous time and the perfect occasion to enjoy what's important to you with those who are. Filling fridges and passing brews to friends was the high point.

Song this recipe is: "Punch You In The Eye."

Show this recipe is: It would be 4/3/98. This beer embodies the spirit of such a wild show. At first the

beer will take you through the corridors of your mind and soul, only to burst into a unique bouquet of ephemeral textures of space resulting in a very beautiful buzz. Of course, by the time you have 3 you'll be doing the tweeprise strut.

Punch You In The IPA

Ingredients:
10 pounds Optic Pale Ale Malt
1 pound Crystal 40L
½ pound Cara-Pils
½ pound Belgian Biscuit Malt
.3 pound Vienna Malt
Chinook hops 11.4% (1 ounce for 60 min)
Cascade hops 6.3% (.75 ounce for 60 min)
Hallertau Hersbruck 3.9% (1 ounce for 15 min)
Irish moss 15 min
Cascade 6.3% (1 ounce for 5 min)
Wyeast American Ale II 1272 yeast

Designed for 5.52 gallons.

Directions:
Mash at 148 F, with hard water. Gypsum was added to replicate the Burton - on - Trent waters. Depending on your water source, more modifications may be needed.

Serves: 20

Drinks

Name: Amy F. Fischer

Location: Albany, NY

Occupation: you name it

Shows Attended: 89 as of end of Fall 2009 tour

Favorite Song: "Divided Sky"

Favorite Experience:
Worcester, MA, Fall 1998 run—I was on tour during college, going to as many shows as I could get away with going to. After the 11/28 Worcester show, I was hanging out with a bunch of tapers in their huge hotel suite, so happy to be getting to know the people that were such an important part of the scene. The music was loud, conversation was interesting, and I was feeling pretty good!
A little while into the partying, I heard that Paul Languedoc was supposed to be stopping by the room shortly. Are you KIDDING?!? Jackpot! I'm going to meet FAMOUS Phish people tonight! Then I heard an hour later that Paul got arrested for loitering in the lobby of our hotel. Shortly after that the cops entered our hotel room.
The next day a Paul & Silas opener! Holy shit! And I actually knew why! For the first time I felt like I was part of a family—a phamily—that created setlists from things that we all experienced together! Hey Paul, can you pass the soap???

Origin of recipe: There's no secret…I just started bringing Bloody Marys to festivals after I heard enough people say there was a need… like when there was a need for a Sammy Smith on lot and no one could find that guy… I liked to pick up the slack.

Favorite memory of sharing recipe:
I had a really late night, no sleep really all weekend, at Camp Bisco 2009. The bikers had busted me a day before for selling liquor, and I had to stop shop or risk being thrown out. My friend Duke loves my Bloody Marys, and I told him no matter what I would make him one that weekend. He was in VIP that weekend, and I for the first time couldn't afford it, so at 8 am, just as I felt like the landing gear was working, Duke texted me and asked if it was at all possible to grab a sacred Bloody Mary before it all ended. I said yes, and pulled myself out of my tent. If someone else is going to want to walk a mile to get one of my Bloody Marys, who am I to deny them!? I made one for each of us, we tapped cups, and discussed all things philosophically appropriate for the last morning at a Camp… no more, and no less.

Amy F'in Fischer's Bloody F'in Marys

Ingredients:
Vodka
Finest Call Bloody Mary Mix (regular, so you can add your own spicy pleasure…)
Green olives with pimientos
Worcestershire sauce
Horseradish
Black pepper
Celery salt
Celery stalks

Directions:
1. Take a 16 ounce cup, fill it halfway with ice.
2. Add two shots of vodka.
3. 1 to 2 healthy shakes of celery salt.
4. 1 to 2 healthy shakes of ground black pepper.
5. Add a dab of horseradish about as large as a pencil top for a weak drink, and as large as a dime for a spicy drink.
6. Add 4 to 6 shakes of Worcestershire sauce.
7. Fill rest of 16 ounce cup with Bloody Mary mix.
8. Stir by pouring into a new cup and back to the old.
9. Garnish with a celery stalk and a toothpick with 2 olives poked through it.

Serves: 1

Name: Terra Pfund and Stephen Kroll

Location: Red Bank, NJ

Occupation: Holistic Health Counselor, Yoga Teacher

Shows Attended: 102

Favorite Song: "Cavern"!!

Favorite Experience: My favorite Phish experience was my 100th show- 8/16/09 at SPAC. I got to go to the show with my boyfriend and love of my life, Stephen, some of my best friends and one of my old tour buddies, Matty. The rainstorm wasn't even a damper on the evening. "David Bowie" into "Cavern" into "Possum" blew my mind and it doesn't get better than a "Harpua" into "I kissed a girl!!!"

Origin of recipe: Red Velvet cake with cream cheese frosting is my absolute favorite cake, but I don't eat it often because of the high fat content, and the artificial coloring scared me a little bit! I started playing around with the recipe to make it a little healthier, using beets for the "food coloring" (which makes a much moister cupcake!).

Favorite memory of sharing recipe: Stephen making a yucky face, closing his eyes to take a bite because he knew they were "healthy" and had beets in them. As soon as he took a bite, his eyes widened and he started

jumping up and down because they were so yummy!

Song this recipe is: "Wading in the Velvet Sea"

Show this recipe is: Oh, 8/16/09 of course…because of the big rain storm…because the cupcakes are moist, creamy and delicious!

Wading in the Velvet Sea Cupcakes

Ingredients:
Cupcakes:
1 ¼ cups spelt flour
1 ¼ cups sugar in the raw
1 ½ tablespoons dark organic cocoa powder
1 ½ teaspoons baking powder
¼ teaspoon salt
¾ cup fresh puréed beets
(3-4 medium sized beets)
⅓ cup oil
(I used Fresh Shores extra virgin coconut oil)
¼ cup lemon juice
1 ½ teaspoons vanilla extract
Frosting:
2- 8 ounce packages cream cheese**
½ cup organic no-salt butter**
2 cups powdered sugar
1 teaspoon organic vanilla extract
Pecans
** You can make this frosting vegan style, simply substitute Tofutti for the dairy cream cheese and Earth Balance spread for the butter

Directions:
Cupcakes:
1. Boil beets in hot water until soft. Scrape/peel the skin off and let cool. Purée the cooked beets along with about 3 or 4 tablespoonss of water, in a blender till smooth. Set aside. You can do this ahead and refrigerate the purée for a day or even freeze it.
2. Sift together the flour, sugar, cocoa, baking powder and salt in a bowl.
3. Put the puréed beets, oil, lemon juice and vanilla extract into another bowl and lightly whisk together till mixed well.
4. Pour this into the bowl with the dry ingredients and mix just enough to combine. Do not over-mix. Divide the batter equally between 12 cupcake tins lined with paper cups.
5. Bake the cupcakes at 350 degrees for about 20 to 25 minutes, until a toothpick comes out clean.
6. Cool completely and decorate with frosting and top with diced pecans.

Frosting:
Cream together butter and cream cheese until just combined. Use a handheld mixer to whip while adding powdered sugar in ½ cup batches. Mix until smooth and creamy, then mix in the vanilla. If frosting is too thick to blend, add a teaspoon or two of milk or soy milk (vegan option) Keep tightly covered and refrigerated until ready to use.

Serves: 12

Name: Greg Bickett

Location: Syracuse, NY

Occupation: Teacher

Shows Attended: 36 at the moment

Favorite Song: "Piper"

Favorite Experience: Sitting the luxury boxes in Hartford when Icculus returned.

Origin of recipe: Personal spin on my adoptive mother Paula Dean's recipe.

Favorite memory of sharing recipe: Pete came to Syracuse to donate PhanArt to Bird Library on the SU Campus. We had a few drinks at Faegan's and attended a lacrosse showdown with Colgate, which SU won handily. I whipped these brownies up and ate one before the game. Pete took the rest with him to a beach party where they won rave reviews.

Blondies With Dreads

Ingredients:
1 cup butter
4- 1 ounce squares white chocolate
¾ cup brown sugar
¾ cup sugar
3 large eggs
1 ½ cups flour
1 teaspoon vanilla
1 cup white chocolate morsels
1 cup chopped macadamia nuts

Directions:
1. Preheat the oven to 350 degrees. Coat a 12 x 18 in. pan with nonstick cooking spray.
2. Combine butter and white chocolate squares in a bowl and microwave on high for 1 minute. Stir. Continue heating in 30 second intervals, stirring after each one, until mixture is melted and smooth.
3. Combine butter mixture and sugars in a large bowl. Add eggs, one at a time, beating well after each one. Gradually stir in flour. Stir in vanilla, white chocolate morsels, and nuts.
4. Spoon batter into prepared pan. Bake until a toothpick comes out clean from the center, about 25 minutes. Cool in the pan and cut into individual portions.

Serves: 18

Name: Michael Lorusso

Location: Chicago, IL

Occupation: Student

Shows Attended: Not many

Favorite Song: "Sparkle"

Favorite Experience: The lightning at Deer Creek '09. You could just see so much lightning off the in distance and it slowly crept up to the stage, all while Phish was playing.

Origin of recipe: My mom has made these and I decided to substitute the normal butter for some alternative butter. Turned out great! Thanks mom!

Favorite memory of sharing recipe: I'm making these for Festival 8, so hopefully they bring some great memories!

Song this recipe is: "Guelah Papyrus"

Show this recipe is: Live At Madison Square Garden, New Year's Eve 1995.

Special Surphrise Cookies

Ingredients:
1 cup packed brown sugar
¾ cup sugar
¾ cup butter
¾ cup peanut butter
2 eggs
1 teaspoon vanilla
2 ½ cups flour
1 teaspoon baking soda
25 chocolate candies (Kit Kats, Peanut Butter Cups, Hershey Chocolate Bars, Mounds) cut in half

Directions:
1. Heat oven to 250 degrees. Combine the brown sugar, sugar and butter in a large bowl. Either use an electric mixer or beat by hand until creamy.
2. Form the dough around the candy and completely cover it. Place 2 inches apart onto ungreased cookie sheets.
3. Bake for 20 to 25 minutes or until golden brown around edges. Let them cool, and enjoy!
* What's cool about this recipe is that each cookie will have a different type of candy. Ahhh, the element of surprise! Yum!

Serves: 20

Name: Erin Berniche

Location: Cape Cod, MA

Occupation: Bartender

Favorite Song: "The Moma Dance"

Favorite Experience: My very first show in VA Beach, summer of '99 is one of my fondest experiences… it felt like coming home.

Origin of recipe: It came together over several years of tasting many interesting homemade creations in the lot and at various festivals. This recipe is delicious, easy to make, and open to interpretation…

Favorite memory of sharing recipe: All the smiles.

Song this recipe is: "Simple"

Gotta Goo-Ball Jibboo

Ingredients:
2 cups of organic crispy brown rice cereal
¼ cup of butterscotch chips
¼ cup of chocolate chips
½ cup of almond butter (or your favorite nut butter)
¼ cup of coconut flakes
½ cup of your favorite (melted) butter
¼ cup of agave nectar

Directions:
1. Mix all of the ingredients and place in the fridge until dough becomes firm enough to work with.
2. Dip your hands in warm water, then roll the mixture into 2 to 3 inch balls and put them on a cookie sheet. Place in the fridge until you are ready to serve them.
3. Get creative by dipping the balls into melted dark chocolate and then rolling in finely crushed walnuts.

Serves: 8

Name: Muffin

Location: Northwest New Jersey/Tour

Occupation: Human

Shows Attended: Well over 100

Favorite Song: Really? No, cannot answer that…

Favorite Experience: Amy's Farm… really, nothing more needs to be said than that!

Origin of recipe: I originally got it in 1990 from a baking soda box and have tweaked it over the years to make it my own as much as possible, and use healthier ingredients and more naners!

Favorite memory of sharing recipe: Every time I bake one, I give it away, so they all are special!

Song this recipe is: "YEM"

Show this recipe is: All of them, because like a Phish show every bread is totally different and never ever are they the same!

Muffin's Nummy 'Nana Bread

Ingredients:
*Mind you, I try to make everything using all organic ingredients, so I won't bother saying organic in every piece, just know it is organic.
4 really ripe bananas, the blacker the better (teehee), MASHED, Sometimes it is nice to have them clumpy, other times I use a ricer to get them like baby food for a nice smooth bread.
1 egg
¼ cup melted butter
A generous splash of apple juice (about a ¼ cup to half, but only use ¼ in the wet ingredients, and use more later if too sticky)
1 ½ cups flour
1 cup sugar (sometimes I use half sugar and half honey or something along those lines, also if you love apple, you could use some apple sauce in place of the sugar)
1 teaspoon baking soda
1 teaspoon salt
Cinnamon to personal taste (depending on the time of year: I love more in fall and winter and just a little in summer)
*If you like, you can use nuts or dried fruit as well, but again depending on time of year I either add tons or nothing!
*Sometimes I sprinkle the top with brown sugar or a granola mix, nuts or dried fruits…it is up to you to make it your own each and every time!
*And last but never least, music (one must dance around the kitchen whilst baking, I believe this has much to do with how great the food ends up tasting!)

(*Recipe continued on page 169*)

Muffin's Nummy 'Nana Bread

(continued)

Directions:

1. Mix the wet ingredients together, being careful with the butter as it can cook the egg if added too quickly or when it is too hot… drizzle it in slowly to warm the wet ingredients.
2. Sift together the flours, sugar, salt, baking soda and cinnamon. Add slowly to the wet, mixing well and not adding too much to create the flour crop dusting of me and my counter!
3. Heat the oven to 350 degrees F…
4. Grease a bread pan (I use the 9 x 5 in. usually, or I think that is the size) with your choice of greaser; I use butter, but PAM or what have you will work well.
5. Once the mix is well-incorporated and smooth, if you notice it seems a bit sticky, or really thick, add a splash of apple juice to thin it a bit…now careful, you don't want it runny, but nice, smooth, and thick is fine.
6. Bake for 65 mins. Once you take it out, check it with a toothpick in the middle. If it comes out clean, it is done. If not, put it in another 5 mins and recheck.

*Sometimes it is fun to experiment with things in these breads, like using coconut flour in place of a bit of the flour, using whole wheat, using apple cider instead of juice, or whatever. This is your bread to have fun with!

Serves: 8

Name: Matthew Malinowski

Location: Buffalo, NY

Occupation: GIS Analyst

Shows Attended: 15

Favorite Song: "David Bowie"

Favorite Experience: My first show, Oswego 1999 Festival, was such an eye-opener. I was pretty much hooked already, but that experience sealed the deal.

Origin of recipe: It popped up in a Fark discussion regarding the two potential first-ladies comparing their recipes. It jumped out at me since I love pumpkin pie and it has been a hit with everyone who has tried them. Thank you, Fark.

Favorite memory of sharing recipe: When I first started dating my fiancée I made a batch of the cookies and shared them with her family. I was well-liked from that point on.

Song this recipe is: "Esther"

Show this recipe is: 10/31/96 because of the Halloween/Pumpkin combination and it's my favorite Halloween show.

Pumpkin Pie Cookies

Ingredients:
1 cup (2 sticks) salted butter, softened
1 cup white sugar
1 cup LIGHT brown sugar
2 large eggs
1 teaspoon vanilla extract
1 cup canned pumpkin purée (not pumpkin pie mix)
3 cups all-purpose flower
2 teaspoons baking soda
1 teaspoon ground cinnamon
½ teaspoon ground ginger
¼ teaspoon ground nutmeg
¼ teaspoon ground cloves
2 cups (1- 12-ounce bag) milk chocolate chips, either sweet or semi-sweet
Nonstick cooking spray

Directions:

1. Heat oven to 350 degrees. Spray cookie sheets with nonstick spray.
2. Using a mixer, beat the butter until smooth. Beat in the white and brown sugars a little bit at a time until the mixture is light and fluffy. Beat in the eggs one at a time then mix in the vanilla and pumpkin purée.
3. In a large bowl, whisk together the flour, baking soda, cinnamon, ginger, nutmeg, and cloves.
4. Slowly beat the flour mixture into the batter in thirds. Stir in the chocolate chips.
5. Scoop the cookie dough in heaping tablespoons onto the prepared cookie sheet and bake 15 to 20 minutes, or until the cookies are browned around the edges. Remove the cookie sheets from the oven and let them rest for 2 minutes. Take the cookies off with a spatula and cool them on wire racks.

Makes approximately 45 to 50 cookies.

Serves: 20

Name: Kat Griffin

Location: Upstate NY mountains

Occupation: Accomplice

Shows Attended: 78ish

Favorite Song: “Divided Sky”

Favorite Experience: The electricity of my first “Divided Sky” at the Weedsport 7/15/93 show, which also was my first show. After listening to their CDs for a few months I needed to know more about this band and who the hell writes a song like “Esther” anyway. Weedsport was small and uncrowded. We bought our tickets in the lot from an official ticket seller wearing a carpenter’s apron and using a roll of carnival-type raffle tickets for the “official” tickets. Bizarro. Fast forward to “Divided Sky.” My jaw was on the ground. I knew I needed more of this magic in my life. Hence began my journey into phishdom, new friends, the mockingbird foundation and more jaw-dropping music. And it was good.

Origin of recipe: Hmmm I do not remember. For years I have made it for assorted bands that have stayed at our house. We do a sort of band bed and breakfast for bands…to give them some home cooking and a break from life on the road. I have been altering it each time I make it.

Favorite memory of sharing recipe: The Hot Buttered Rum String Band boys drooling over it at our dining room table.

Song this recipe is: “Split Open and Melt”

Show this recipe is: Sunrise set at Big Cypress.

Kat's Orgasmic Blooberry Streusel To Die For

Ingredients:
¼ cup softened (not melted) butter plus 6 tablespoons.
¾ cup sugar
1 egg
2 cups flour plus 6 tablespoons
½ teaspoon salt
2 teaspoons baking powder
½ cup milk
2 cups blueberries
1 cup packed light brown sugar
4 teaspoons cinnamon
1 cup chopped pecans or walnuts (optional)

Directions:
1. Cream together ¼ cup softened (not melted) butter, ¾ cup sugar, and 1 egg.
2. Mix together 2 cups flour, ½ teaspoon salt, 2 teaspoons baking powder, ½ cup milk.
3. Add flour mixture to butter mixture and gently blend. The batter will be thick and gloopy.
4. Spoon into well greased 13 x 9 cake pan. I bloop it around then sort of pat it down to fit the pan…it really doesn't want to be spread like a regular thin batter.
5. Scatter 2 cups blueberries that have been patted dry on top of the batter and gently press them in.
6. Mix together 1 cup packed light brown sugar, 6 tablespoons flour, 4 teaspoons cinnamon, 6 tablespoons soft butter, 1 cup chopped pecans or walnuts (optional) sprinkle on top of batter.
*Note: The streusel topping is thick and gloopy as well. If a more crumbly topping is desired, add a bit more flour and some white sugar to the topping mixture.
*Optional: Sprinkle the topping in the pan with ⅛ to ¼ cup of turbinado sugar, that light, brownish, big-crystaled, chunky, sparkly sugar. This adds a wonderful crispyish, crunchyish-ness to the streusel.
7. Bake in 375 degree oven for 35 to 40 minutes. Test for doneness after 35 minutes.
8. Dish yourself out a big hunk o' this stuff generously slathered with butter. Pour a glass of ice cold milk… and ascend.

Serves: 8

Name: Lindsay Jones

Location: Utica, NY

Occupation: Underwriter

Shows Attended: 27

Favorite Song: "Carini"

Favorite Experience: My roadtrip to Alpine Valley this year!

Origin of recipe: My Mom!

Favorite memory of sharing recipe: It's my go-to cookie, it has everything in it, and I make it a lot!

Multibeast Cookies

Ingredients:
3 eggs
1 ¼ cups packed brown sugar
1 cup sugar
1 tablespoon Karo syrup (I use light)
¾ teaspoon vanilla
1 12-ounce jar chunky peanut butter
1 stick butter, softened, not melted
1 cup M&M's
½ cup chocolate chips
¼ cup Reeses Pieces
2 teaspoons baking soda
4 ½ cups oatmeal

Directions:

1. Heat oven to 350 degrees.
2. Mix together eggs and sugars using a mixer.
3. Add salt, butter, vanilla, and peanut butter.
4. Stir in the candy/chocolate chips, baking soda, and oatmeal.
5. Drop by tablespoons, 2 inches apart, since they get big.
6. Bake for 8 to 10 minutes.

Serves: 20

Name: Adam Lebin & Malaika Marion

Location: Chicago, Il. *The Brown Sack Soup, Sandwich & Shake Shack*

Occupation: Restaurant Owner

Shows Attended: 90 Plus?

Favorite Song: "Col. Forbin's Ascent"

Favorite Experience: Being in the first five rows at Alpine Valley 1997. Still an all time favorite show of mine. The boys were on fire for the entire show. Every song was taken to another level.

Origin of recipe: We serve this cornbread at our sandwich shop in Chicago.

Favorite memory of sharing recipe: It's great having people come into the restaurant and seeing our phish posters on the wall and then being blown away by the quality and uniqueness of our menu.

Song this recipe is: "Colonel Forbin's Ascent" because it's hot and sweet!

Show this recipe is: Alpine Valley 1997, a show that was hot from top to bottom with a sweet set list. Just like the cornbread which is savory, hot in the middle and sweet on top.

Colonel Forbin's Jalapeño & Honey Cornbread

Ingredients:
5- 8.5 ounces boxes of Jiffy Corn Muffin Mix
5 eggs
1 ⅓ cups of whole milk
1 whole jalapeño
Butter for greasing cooking dishes.
2 dishes (we prefer earthenware) measuring 11 x 7.5 inches with a depth of 1 ¾ inches

Directions:

1. Dice the jalapeño, stems and seeds included, as small as possible.
2. Crack 5 eggs into a medium size bowl.
3. Measure out 1 ⅓ cups of whole milk.
4. Combine these three ingredients in bowl and whisk until eggs are completely mixed.
5. Add all 5 boxes of Jiffy Corn Muffin Mix and whisk until smooth.
6. Split the contents of bowl into 2 earthenware dishes measuring 11 x 7.5 in. and about 1 ¾ inches deep.
7. Cook at 325 degrees for around 35 minutes or until top is a nice golden brown.
8. Remove from oven. Squeeze honey on top of each pan of cornbread and spread over the top.
9. Allow to cool for ½ hour.

Serves: 12

Name: Brooke Nuckles

Location: Vermont

Occupation: Artist and Teen Outreach Worker

Shows Attended: 17

Favorite Song: "Lizards"

Favorite Experience: Blossom 2000 the last show of the mini fall tour. Good times.

Origin of recipe: Evolved after years of trial and tribulations. Experimentations, police confrontations, destiny unbound stipulations, humboldt county manifestations…

Favorite memory of sharing recipe: At the Gorge, passing out next to my basket o' brownies marked with one-of-a-kind sparkle sign, and waking up with a half-body sunburn, a big old smile and a basket of cash.

Song this recipe is: "I Am Hydrogen"

Show this recipe is: Hershey Park 2000- chocolate world! YAY! Or, Trey Merriweather Post Pavillion, summer 2001: crafty ladies made a bundle selling a trunk full of these bad boys and Stichin' Bitches threads- Yeeah!

One Of A Kind Brownies

Ingredients:
Your choice of Butter
Brownie mix
Egg
Bonus ingredients:
Chocolate chips
Nuts
Peanut butter (and jelly!)

Directions:
Betty Crocker style (follow directions on the box):
1. Mix it
2. Love it
3. Bake it
4. Eat it/sell it/give 'em away!!!!!

Serves: 20

Name: Carol Huffman

Location: West Granby, CT

Occupation: A Mom McLovin

Shows Attended: 1 (but it was Hartford, 2009)

Favorite Song: "Backwards Down the Numberline"

Favorite Experience: Hanging out with Patrick & the guys at WaterWheel, all of the new friendships and musical journeys.

Origin of recipe: It's quite a CONUNDRUM really.

Favorite memory of sharing recipe: I make cookies for McLovin band practices. Once I used a teaspoon to form the indentation (instead of my thumb). Jason went crazy on me because he said they were INDUSTRIAL cookies and no longer pure. I've used my thumb ever since.

Song this recipe is: "YEM"

Show this recipe is: Hartford, because it is the best :D

McLovin Jams

Ingredients:
2 sticks unsalted butter
1 cup sugar
¼ teaspoon salt
1 tablespoon really good vanilla (like Madagascar or Baldwin)
2 cups all purpose flour
Some Jam of your choice. Jake, Jason and Jeff are partial to raspberry, but they also enjoyed Stonewall Kitchen's Strawberry Brandied Apricot.

Directions:

1. Preheat oven to 325 degrees.
2. In a medium bowl, beat the butter, sugar, salt and vanilla until combined.
3. Add flour slowly on a low speed or mix by hand.
4. Line your cookie sheets with parchment paper.

*I use a small cookie scoop to measure the dough, then roll it and place on the parchment (leaving room for the spread). Indent each dough ball using YOUR THUMB and fill with Jam.

5. Bake about 20 minutes.
6. Cool a little and enjoy!

Serves: 14

Name: Greg Bickett

Location: Syracuse, NY

Occupation: Teacher

Shows Attended: 36 not counting November '09

Favorite Song: "Piper"

Favorite Experience: Hitting up most of the Summer '99 tour with Matty B. playing Yahtzee in the center console of Matt's car while driving across a bridge in Maryland on the way to Camden.

Origin of recipe: I love putting my own touch on the classic recipe. For this batch, I simply opened up the freezer and incorporated all of the chocolate I could find in there.

Favorite memory of sharing recipe: Darien Lake 2009. Large group of friends from all parts of my life sampled them before heading into the show.

Show this recipe is: I guess it would be the Darien show since that's where they were eaten. They did enhance the Darien Jam in many special ways.

Triple Chocolate Rice Krispy Treats

Ingredients:
4 ounces butter
1 bag of mini marshmallows
3 cups Rice Krispies
3 cups Cocoa Krispies
1 cup semisweet chocolate chips
1 milk chocolate candy bar, chopped
1 dark chocolate candy bar, chopped

Directions:
1. Spray a 12 x 8 inch pan with nonstick cooking spray.
2. Melt the butter over low heat in a large kettle.
3. Add marshmallows and stir constantly until the mixture is melted together.
4. Remove from the heat and add in the Krispies.
5. Stir to coat the Krispies with the mixture.
6. Add in the chocolate chips and chopped candy bars and stir to combine.
7. Quickly spoon the sticky mixture into the pan.
8. Press the mass into the pan using a piece of wax paper, making sure it is evenly distributed.
9. Refrigerate until cool.
10. Cut and serve.

Serves: 18

Name: Britin Foster

Location: Albany, NY

Occupation: Baker

Shows Attended: 1! First this year.

Favorite Song: "Alaska"

Favorite Experience: Well, I've only had one so far in Albany in September but it blew my mind and I look forward to more!

Origin of recipe: This recipe came from a whole winter of experimentation to make the perfect chocolate chip cookie!

Britin's Best Vegan Chocolate Chip Cookies

Ingredients:
1 ½ cup sifted flour
½ cup quick oats
1 teaspoon baking soda
½ cup Earth Balance, soy butter
¼ cup peanut butter, salted, creamy
½ cup brown sugar
½ cup raw sugar
½ teaspoon vanilla extract
¼ cup soymilk, unsweetened
¾ cup dark vegan chocolate chips

Directions:
1. In a small bowl, sift flour with soda, salt and oats.
2. In a large bowl, cream butters together, then gradually add sugars and mix well.
3. Add vanilla and mix.
4. Blend in sifted ingredients alternately with the milk, starting and ending with dry mixture.
5. Stir in chocolate chips.
6. Drop by full teaspoon onto ungreased cookie sheet.
7. Bake at 350 degrees for 10 to 12 minutes until just golden brown.

Makes 12 large cookies or 24 small.

Index

Interested in submitting your own recipe to PHANFOOD?

Follow the link to submit your recipe for the next edition of PhanFood.